Why
Can't I
Believe?

Why Can't I Believe?

Struggling with Faith and Doubt

GAYLORD NOYCE

Chalice Press®
St. Louis, Missouri

Cover art: Les Wright
Cover design: Elizabeth Wright
Interior design: Elizabeth Wright

This book is printed on acid-free, recycled paper.

Visit Chalice Press on the World Wide Web at
www.chalicepress.com

10 9 8 7 6 5 4 3 2 1   99 00 01 02 03

Library of Congress Cataloging–in–Publication Data

Noyce, Gaylord B.
    Why can't I believe? / by Gaylord Noyce.
          p.   cm.
    ISBN 0-8272-4241-7
    1. Christian life. 2. Imaginary conversations.   I. Title.
    BV4501.2.N69   1999   99–38105
    248.4—dc21   CIP

Printed in the United States of America

CONTENTS

Introduction: Finding the Way to Christian Faith   1

1   Darkness: A Visit with Sophie   3

2   First Questions: A Visit with Newt   11

3   Messed Up: A Visit with Elsena   21

4   Truth: A Visit with Newt   27

5   Law: A Visit with Linda   37

6   Scripture and Dogma: A Visit with Newt   47

7   Kindness: A Visit with Elsena   55

8   What about Jesus? A Visit with Newt   63

9   A Letter to Newt   73

10 Jesus Christ: A Visit with Newt   81

11 At Sea: A Visit with April   91

12 Evil: A Visit with Newt   99

13 Relinquishment: A Visit with Sophie   105

14 Buddha: A Visit with Newt   115

15 Justice: A Visit with Rafer   123

16 Grace: A Visit with Linda   131

17 Prayer: A Visit with Newt   137

18 Picnic: A Visit with Everyone   145

INTRODUCTION

Finding the Way to
Christian Faith

You and I live in a time of religious ferment. The urban land-scape now mixes mosques and temples with churches and syna-gogues, and without fanfare, spiritually oriented groups meet in meditation and conference rooms, retreat centers and fancy ho-tels. Their texts cover everything from AA to Zen.

Among the people involved in this new spirituality are people who want to believe but can't. They drop off their children at Sun-day school and think for a moment about staying for church them-selves, before going home for morning chores or the Sunday supplement. Or they do stay, sitting in the back pews. But they have trouble *believing*.

In this book I want to help people think about some of that. We will work through hesitations and barriers that hinder the re-ligious quest. We employ a time-honored method for this—the dialogue. Baker, the counselor/minister who is a resource for our seekers, hopes to serve as a midwife for believing. Baker may be a more experienced Christian than they but is by no means their better.

This is a book of pastoral apologetics. Its locale is the bound-ary region between the secular world and the traditional territory of Christian faith. Internal matters of coherence and implication are to be found elsewhere.

Such seekers as we deal with bring with them lively questions and troubled faces. Their need is sometimes for little more than listening on Baker's part and for a measure of care. But occasionally the discussions shift and the shuttled exchange creates a rich fabric reminiscent of the probing conversation in a good novel, or even of classic dialogues like those in Job or Plato.

These conversations are not transcriptions. They are composites of parishioner/seekers, my own struggles toward belief, and the multiple yearnings and disenchantments of our secular culture. Idealized as they are, they derive from human experience as real as the hard tiles on my bathroom floor.

1

Darkness:
A Visit with Sophie

"I believe; help my unbelief." Mark 9:24

Sophie comes with twin questions: "What are we to do when it seems God is not there?" and, "How can faith leave us when we had thought it was secure?" She is forty-three, the mother of three, and facing new limits to her once-buoyant life. Pleasantries past, she begins with her state of spirit.

(Sophie) I can't say easily just what is wrong. It's nothing very specific. What I know is that I don't seem to get much out of church anymore. Time was when I got a lot from it. God was really "there" when I prayed. Now there is nothing there. No one. I was once buoyed up by Sunday services. I went home with a song in my heart. And it's not that way any more. God is gone. There's no song. I want to believe, but I can't.

(Baker) And what gets in your way?

That's it. Nothing "gets in the way." There is just no energy to believe with. Sometimes I get scared in the night. But mostly it's just the emptiness. How can I once have believed so much and then have lost it?

You did believe and now it's gone—that faith.

Yes. It's like marriage—the romance fades away and you're left with only the skeleton of it, the formal ties but no passion, no spontaneity in love. In love, a lot of the fading is probably hormones. So you can make some sense of it, but faith ought to be more than that. By definition, it's what you depend on when all else fails you. So did I never have true faith?

> Suppose it's the same in belief—in the natural scheme of things? The religious passion of youth wanes, too, the mountaintop experiences, that burning zeal for Christ?

I have thought about that. You may be right. But my experience this winter has been more serious, more depressing. Everything is going downhill. I feel empty, absolutely empty. Nothing sings anymore. I see the daffodils and my heart does not leap up. I saw a child's smile yesterday, and I wasn't moved. I want more out of life than survival. I am all dried up.

> I see. Despair, not just discouragement. There's no spring left to heal your winter.

Exactly. Maybe it's the "long dark night of the soul" I have heard people talk about. It's long and dark, at any rate. It's night and I can't sleep. (I wish I could!) Do you have any suggestions?

> Tell me about yourself, Sophie. I don't know you all that well.

My life? That isn't a big order. A pretty ordinary life.

I suppose you want to know if there are events that would be sapping my religious life. There are plenty, but they're no worse than what I've dealt with before. No worse than others' problems.

I'm forty-three. I've had all my children. Three of them. My husband—you've met Roger, I think—is faithful and good and doing well, although he's coming to realize he won't ever be president— president of the firm, that is. In fact, he thinks sometimes about quitting and going into some crazy thing like school teaching or setting up a little lab for himself. He calls those times his "better mousetrap" days, when he thinks he can do anything, and the world will come to his door. Sherry, our oldest, is about to go off to college. And the other two are close behind. That's about it.

> And you're in good health?

Yes—I had a physical last month. It's not a physical sickness, I'm sure. And my gynecologist tells me to wait it out, it's not menopause yet. She, too, insists I'm in good physical health.

I took on the job at the library anticipating the college bills—I've been saving a little every month for almost three years now. I wasn't trained for anything special. English major, married right after college. The kids came along, and they were often sick, and we didn't have any money. That's why I said it has been worse other years. But everything wasn't so bleak as it is now. There's no relief any more. No humor, no lightness. Nothing is spacious; things seem to close in. It got worse a few months ago when Roger's sister died. She left three children, all preteen. That was awful. I remember thinking God was a hit-and-run driver. Absconded. Left the scene.

But yes. I'm in good health.

> I imagine you would prefer it were a sickness you could name. Is there any relief, ever?

Not really. Oh, it comes and goes a little. It's worse when I'm lonely. I get to feeling I don't have a friend in the world.

> That is a desperate feeling, that bleakness. Tell me, when faith was strong, was God a friend, or someone far away in the cosmos unconnected to you?

I wasn't this way before. I didn't seem to have any trouble believing. I went to church and I was even a Sunday school teacher, although not an especially good one, I am sure. God? God was a friend, who seemed to guarantee that every problem was surmountable. God was a source of energy. I could talk to God, and I did, often.

> But no more?

I guess I lost faith gradually. Life got busier with the children—in a secular way. And with social things in town. We stopped being so regular at bedtime prayers with the children and grace at meals. The first two children were confirmed, and they promptly balked at attending church. Roger and I stopped, too, and had some great free weekends as a result.

But I don't equate churchgoing to faith, do you?

No. I don't. Why do you ask?

I suppose I feel a little guilty. But what good is church if you can't believe?

> For some people—people who think they don't believe much—church may mean that they know they need God even if they don't have the firsthand experience anymore. That may seem strange to you. They search for God in worship. They try to affirm God. For others who also don't go in much for God-talk or liturgy, the church reinforces moral energy. They want to be better people and to serve the community. Church seems to represent that intention. It seems to help with that. Actually I guess neither kind qualifies as what you are thinking of as believers. They have little sense of God's being in the room with them, you might say. They don't feel like they've arrived at faith. Yet, there they are in church, trusting, I believe, that there will yet be a revelation of more.
>
> Excuse my meandering. In your dark shadows, the last thing you want is argument from me.

No. I want hope. But I think I see a point in what you say. Those people have hope. And they work at it in their own ways. I haven't been very intentional about my faith. Maybe God has tired of me. I didn't work at it. I just felt God would keep coming into my life anyway—as he did—or she did—when I was a teenager. I didn't give it much thought.

> Of course you were partly right. We can't manufacture faith—ultimately. Faith is a lot like love. Love needs a certain spontaneity, a certain abandon, or it isn't love. I am attracted to my beloved, so I say, "I love you."

Faith did come that way in my childhood. It seemed as natural and beautiful as a sunset at the beach or the excitement of Christmas. But so many things chisel away at it as you grow. In the end it was like believing in Santa Claus. I've grown out of it.

> You mean Santa Claus was a childish illusion. And are you saying faith was like that? It simply stopped working? At least you had to put away a childish understanding, or it would stop working?

Yes, I suppose I should have abandoned childish ways of believing. But I'm not sure I've done that yet. I may have been just coasting on the childhood momentum. Sometimes they're a comfort though. You know I still go to sleep sometimes with the "Now I-lay-me" prayer. Is that wrong?

At least that may be part of my emptiness—I still long for that childhood innocence in believing. I suppose I have to grow up more.

> Maybe there are things that can help. I was leading up to a second thought when I spoke of love. We think of love as coming spontaneously. We expect to be swept off our feet. But Jesus also commanded us to work at it—"Love your neighbor," he said. That asks obedience, not exuberance.

I have been passive, I guess, thinking the belief thing would take care of itself. I should have prayed more. But now my despair doesn't lend itself to working at anything. It doesn't prompt action. It condemns me to lethargy. I'm a spiritual hypochondriac. I gripe and do nothing to manage my health. If it's possible, how would you work at faith at my age, in my situation of darkness?

> Let me ask what has been most meaningful to you in times past? I can't write you a prescription. After all, there have been many different paths in devotion—from the mystics and the contemplatives to the spiritual activists like Martin Luther King, or Martin Luther himself.

I've gone through phases. When I was young, being with the group was the big thing. We had a Young Life group, a period of Bible study with an athletic leader whom all the girls adored. Because of my family, I made my circle even more tight and rigid. We didn't go to Sunday movies, speak four letter words, use make-up. That's OK, and it probably kept us from ruining our lives in some cases. But it lacked much depth, in spite of all of us saying we had been saved from sin by Jesus our Lord. We didn't study the Bible, I don't think; we memorized certain words and phrases, that's all.

Then I had my long, long thoughts period, when solitude seemed holy, and the crowd—even at church—was the intrusion. Those were wonderful times. Everything was "Kodachrome." Life was full. God was in heaven, and it never seemed to rain.

Then Roger; then the children. It all went pretty fast.

Where would you begin if you were to do it all over?

I simply don't know. Of course, I've tried prayer. But as I say, there's no one there now when I pray. Going to church anymore would seem like hypocrisy, because I would be pretending. I am lost, that's all. I've even thought of running to live elsewhere, as if it were a matter of place. Here, God is gone.

> Sophie, you speak with a serious-minded energy. I find it hard to think of you as spiritually washed-up. You want more out of life than emotional drought and cerebral detachment. Unlike some people, you know you're empty. A car without a fuel gauge is a lot more likely to run out of gas. You know life is meant to be more. You are not a cynic.

Maybe. But that doesn't comfort me. Do other people reach this point?

> You're not the only one, if that is what you are asking. But I doubt that that comforts you either. A person's own pain is always unique.

I am really at my wit's end. I dreamed the other night that I was a young girl and my little red tricycle had been lost—or stolen. I didn't know which. And I was inconsolable. I woke up crying, actually. What, in God's name, am I going to do? Do you have any suggestions?

> There is plenty of counsel about waiting patiently—in the psalms, in the mystics. To help you along that way you might try a discipline and stick to it. But you should do it as an experiment. In my experience, if you think of it as a mechanism that works for you for the sake of getting results, or a chore you are compelled to do against your better judgment, it's unlikely to help much. If you think of it as an effort to put yourself in a place more available to God and the spirit, you might be helped.

What do you mean by a discipline?

> An intentional, regular practice. You could read in theology, for example, because of your comments about growing up—or you could read scripture. Alone, or with others. We could then

talk further. You can be more deliberate about meditation, or reading the great prayers—starting, perhaps, with the simpler psalms. This won't bring you out of the dark night, but it might inch you toward the light, to mix metaphors.

Come back if you like after a week—or a month—and we will talk some more.

Thank you. I'm not ready for a group. Perhaps I will try scripture—again. I've done that before, you know. What should I read?

I could suggest a serious-minded slow reading of a psalm—perhaps Psalm 139—daily. It won't necessarily bring God near. Just read it. Out loud would be good. Do that over and over. That psalm has in it an expression that might help you: "The darkness is as light to you"—addressed to God. And along with that, start working your way through a gospel—you pick your favorite. And don't hurry it. Savor what is meaningful. And we'll talk about it.

You won't rediscover your faith directly out of this exercise. And I won't be glib with *bon mots* or things like "It is always darkest before the dawn." It's dark before bad storms too. All I can say is that there are others who have been where you are. The Psalms are full of laments like yours. And they give many reasons for the darkness—sometimes it's even God's own purposive withdrawal from the human scene.

I guess God abandoned some of them too.

Let's talk more soon.

Discussion Questions for Chapter 1

1. Sophie said that by definition, faith is "What you depend on when all else fails you." How would you react to those who say Sophie lacked true faith or this would not have happened to her?

2. Sophie's problems, she says, are "No worse than what I've dealt with before." What do you imagine those problems were? Do you see anything different in Sophie's situation now than in the past?

3. How would you characterize your own low times? Do they match Sophie's, when she says there's "no humor, no lightness. Nothing is spacious; things seem to close in?"

4. In your mind, how would you argue whether Sophie needed psychological help or spiritual direction?
5. What good is church if you can't believe?
6. Why does Baker seem to resist suggesting a discipline? Have you found disciplines to be helpful in your own case?
7. Why can't Sophie believe?

2

First Questions:
A Visit with Newt

Newt is an engineer, set on careful analysis, wary of sloppy work and slick answers, honest as the day is long, and a would-be believer.

(Newt) Put it this way: I would like to believe, but I simply can't. All too little about Christian belief makes any sense to me. You might think that was all there is to it. No one forces me to hang around here or talk with religious people. I could just go away. But it troubles me that I don't believe.

> (Baker) You're certainly welcome to hang around, as you put it. You know that.

I thought maybe you could help. Nothing would please me more just now, if you could. What do you think?

> Maybe. Maybe not. I have no magic formula for believing.

> I think there's a mystery in believing. Faith is not, in the first instance, anything we do. It's not a human achievement. It can arrive, unbidden, like an unexpected package from the parcel service. Unlike most parcels, of course, this gift has the potential of turning your life around.

Do you mean I can do nothing on my own?

Almost nothing. Faith is a matter of trusting an ultimate ground of confidence or hope, and then framing a way of life appropriate to that confidence.

But you can't conjure up that ground on your own. We simply come to recognize it.

Whoa, back up. You're telling me to go away, find a nice tree to sit under, and wait to be given faith? That's not very satisfying. It's certainly not heroic.

Don't get me wrong. There is struggle, like Jacob's contest when he wrestled all night long with the angel of God, if you remember. It was the time Jacob was terribly afraid because he had to face Esau the next morning. He had cheated Esau out of his inheritance. You've probably had times like that yourself. I have.

Haven't I! That's why I asked to come over here. I've been there with Jacob in the night, scared it wouldn't ever get to be morning. I have felt like a small child lost in the darkening woods during a rain, terrified of what, I don't know—that a tree would fall on me or that the earth would open beneath my feet, panicked that no one could ever find me, wanting my mother, or father, or someone to come rescue me, reorient me, and comfort me. I've also endured moments when everything seemed to have gone sour— my work pointless, my friendships weak, my worth corrupted.

If, as you say, you haven't a faith to comfort you, what does sustain you? I would be deeply interested to know. You don't impress me as especially insecure. I'm interested because whenever I ask that of myself, I do sense an underlying power holding me up. I think of it as God's sustaining regard or guardianship; I have little other way of putting it. So I'm interested: What—would you say—gives you a sense of well-being and purpose?

Even when I feel isolated and uncared for? Let me think about that. Certainly, I would say other people, some friends, their respect for me. Then, too, my physical and mental health are grounds for encouragement. I'm not going hungry. I'm not depressed, no more than the world's serious problems and our own mortality would make me to be. I think I would name music, too. It's comforting, and inspiring, and it seems to say there is more than meets the eye in what is real about the world.

But there are those other times still—often—I feel at odds with everything, wishing for a rudimentary security to stave off the panic.

> Yes, but don't think the believer doesn't also wish for more. "Now we see only darkly, as in a bad mirror, but one day 'face to face.'" That was Saint Paul, loosely translated.

> Actually, I think that in itself is part of the gift—this yearning for deeper understanding of the source and end of life. It's a kind of homesickness.

> So much of what we think sustains us is so transient—friends, health, even those sunlit woods. We seem to need a sense of what endures beneath all that, don't you think? Or the ability, perhaps we should say, to see—right there within the transient— the signs of what truly endures, signs of God.

Yes, but so much seems to signify the demonic, instead. How can the transient become a sign of what endures?

> Good question. But it happens. We do find the signs. No, you're right. Only the believers find signs that much. For others it is often demonic. Maybe that's the audacity of the incarnation— our Christian assertion that in the transient human life of Jesus, we find God among us.

Maybe. But I'm serious. What makes you find—in the transient— God rather than the demonic?

> I'm not sure. Perhaps it's temperament. But I believe it's even more—paradoxically both a choice I make, and a gift I receive.

> I know people do seem to devote themselves to the demonic, and to transient values—wealth, fame, power—that are not true signs of God. They are "graven images," inadequate gods.

> Our human willpower manipulates things seen, heard, felt, or smelled. But faith in God is something else. God is not visible, or audible, or tangible. Trust in God can't be willed, as much as one can wish for it.

So, are you saying there is nothing I can do?

The things you can do won't guarantee you security, or hope, or purpose. If it were that simple, I would not have called faith a gift. It would be something we achieve by what we do. The Holy would be at our beck and call, manipulable. God would be at the end of a psychological process we undertake or of a syllogism we create. We can neither dream up Christian faith nor reason it up. We can't buy it or legislate it.

We can do this. We can take seriously our hunger for dimensions of living that are deeper than our culture's ideas of achievement. Lonely as we feel, many others do share that same hunger. Once we admit the yearning, we've taken a step of faith. Your own first question carries within it the seeds of faith.

That's hopeful. I think I have had hunches about that, but I haven't put it into words very well.

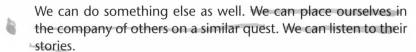

We can do something else as well. We can place ourselves in the company of others on a similar quest. We can listen to their stories.

For example, the alcoholic has to admit the power of addiction and stop denying the problem. Then healing may begin. Usually a gathered company of recovering alcoholics is necessary, Alcoholics Anonymous, people who share their stories. Similarly, hitting bottom spiritually may be our route to faith. "I'm lost. Please, God, find me." And one way God finds us is through the stories shared among believers gathered in community.

Stories?

Like the AA members, Christian people tell stories of religious experience. They share their own accounts of being lost, or troubled, and of being found, or guided, or changed. In particular, they rehearse the accounts of those people whose experiences reverberate throughout scripture and the whole history of the community—Jacob and David and Ruth and Job, Magdalene and Mary and, of course, Jesus himself. Listening to the stories helps us catch on to a view of things profoundly different from a self-centered or material-centered worldview. When theological God-talk wears thin and seems all hollow, remember that theology rests on human experience.

Hearing stories of religious experience may open the way for the gift.

Stories don't seem to me like answers to questions. Maybe you could tell me one of the stories.

> Out of hundreds of them, here's an old one, as well as I remember it. "Moses was keeping the flock of his father-in-law, Jethro, the priest of Midian; and he led his flock to Horeb, the mountain of God. And the angel of the Lord appeared to him in a flame of fire out of the midst of a bush, and he looked, and strangely, the bush was burning. Yet it was not consumed. And Moses said, 'I will turn aside and see this amazing thing, why the bush is not burnt.' God then called to him out of the bush, 'Moses, Moses!' And Moses said, 'Here am I.' Then he said, 'Do not come near; put off your shoes from your feet, for the ground on which you are standing is holy ground.'" That would be in early Exodus.
>
> And as the story goes on, in spite of Moses' resistance, God calls him to liberate the chosen people from pharaoh. That's one of the stories in Jewish and Christian lore.

And that, you see, is the kind of magic that you accept and I cannot believe in. You people amaze me. Intelligent and knowledgeable enough, you still cling to these old fairy tales.

> That story troubles you?

It should trouble you as well. Bushes don't burn without being burnt.

> Of course. Christians know that, too. The point of the story is not its literal absurdity, although some people do, I suppose, take a nature miracle like this as history. And more people once did, I suppose, before the days of natural science. But the point is in the dimension of the holy that the story expresses. Don't you find that here? Holy ground. Put off your shoes. God's speaking, "I am the God of your fathers,…of Abraham, Isaac, and Jacob." There's a lot more. "Moses hid his face, for he was afraid to look at God." God telling Moses he has seen the Israelites' affliction, God sending Moses for their liberation.

But what use is a story based on a false legend? I don't get it.

> The story—this "fairy tale" or "legend " as you call it, and the hundreds of others in the Bible provides the Christian community

with its basic language. The stories form a fabric for our common life in a way that scientific or even philosophical description could never do.

But what can they do except mislead people into a naive prescientific worldview?

I guess that for the stories to be meaningful, you need resources that you don't have just now. You have to neglect the "facts" long enough to hear the story in other dimensions. You have to step into the Bible's world of myth and legend and amazement at God and the given universe so you can stand in awe with Moses.

Does a religion have to include miracle stories that people like me can't believe?

You wouldn't think so, would you? But all religions seem to. At least they have stories that go beyond philosophical proposi-tions. Basically, they present stories about the way the world is, and on that foundation arises a community that rehearses the story in rites of some kind. And those three things—the stories, the rite, and the community—all naturally foster a communal ethic of some sort, a way of living that is appropriate to the story.

Interesting.

It may be paradoxical, but the bulk of the biblical stories do not center on a human "quest" for God, by logic or otherwise. In a sense, the protagonist in the Bible, behind all the narratives of Israel's history, is God. On the surface, the stories tell us about ordinary people. They focus on tangled and sometimes even bloody ways of the community that believed itself called by God for religious ends. The New Testament derives from Jesus, in whom people saw God at work, and on the startup of the church.

But we humans invent the whole array of stories! Stories that claim to be reporting on the work of God, or to be God's very speech to us.

Well, yes, if you choose to put it that way. But even though scripture and religion are products of human hands and souls and minds, believers are not content to say that we humans create the experience of God. All these things respond to and report on that experience. Certainly, we profoundly color the experience in all kinds of ways with our cultural filters and blinders; we have no other language. But the stories point to more than their human authorship. They also point to God's power and ultimacy.

So you say I can do something after all. If I can't create belief on my own, I can, nonetheless, place myself in the community of story-tellers. That doesn't seem like much. Hearing stories isn't what I want when visit a church. I want belief. I want faith. *the stories are experiences of faith, belief.*

Of course. You want to know and trust God. But I won't engineer that personal knowledge and that trust. I can't. I suppose we could brainwash people, if we wanted, trick them into saying they believe, but I believe that would do more harm than good. It would leave us diminished, like robots. It would leave us as shallow believers. That's why doubts are so acceptable as part of your belief.

You say I should join the storytellers because I might catch on. I might receive the gift. You must have more suggestions than that.

Maybe. First let me add to what I said about the company you might walk with. It isn't simply being there to hear what people have once believed. It's the walking itself. We usually think action follows thought-out intent. But action often comes first. Thought can come after. You smile and then you feel happy. The muscles begin to think and feel. If you behave with courtesy, your very disposition toward others takes on a courteous nature. Walking with Christian people, frail as their faith is, you may begin absorbing a Christian sense of yourself. When even that little happens, you're on the way.

You mean that I could settle in among people in church without believing the creed?

Many, many do just that. I would say most Christians came that route. Here's a story. There was a motorcycle club that would always go to a quaint hilltop cafe for Sunday lunch, at least once, early when the spring had come. It was a close-knit group, enjoying the scenery, each other, and the lunch. One of the people at lunch, however, stayed behind as the club members roared off in their procession. He replied, when a tourist asked about this, that he didn't have a motorcycle. He came, driving his old jalopy, to enjoy the club. He found himself welcome; he gradually learned to use all the bikers' jargon; he was learning to be a cyclist and a mechanic. He didn't know whether to call himself a club member or not, but there he was. I don't think he's a full member, not yet.

So I could honestly join before I have worked it all out?

Absolutely. You would find many like you. Some are "members," I guess and some aren't. You would probably find that some would-be believers are deacons and elders and bishops, even. They commit themselves to the company of seekers, without feeling they have arrived at a full-fledged faith. One person's belief in God can be quite unlike another's, even when their language is identical. One person's agreement with the creed may be more socially coerced than another's. Saying a creed may or may not have in it much trust in God.

Doesn't that lead to a lot of hypocrisy?

It surely leaves the way open to it. Actually I have found surprisingly little in my experience—unless expressing good intentions and failing to achieve them is hypocrisy. That kind of failure is part of the human condition universally.

You give me food for thought. But it still seems to me you're dodging my questions about belief. Church people are all right. Many are strong in character and clever and generous. It's their language of doctrine that I can't get my head around. Much of it is nonsense.

I don't mean to dodge any issues you want to work on. We'll have to get to doctrine another day, to what you call nonsense.

For now, let's try one thing more. Let's try asking questions that experiment with answers. Consider the possibility that our very desire to believe is a divine prodding that urges us to trust in holy ground. God has been called the "hound of heaven," pursuing us "down the nights and down the days." A saint said the creator has made our hearts restless until they are at rest in God. If all that is true, you've been moved a good distance on the way of faith already. You simply don't experience it that way or call it faith. You call it unbelief.

I would suggest that faith begins with a holy nudge of hunger after God, and that you know that is beginning, or you wouldn't be here.

Could you spell that out a little further?

I guess I'm urging you to be attentive, not only to the stories and testimony of believers, but also to your own doubts. Treat them with respect. Don't coercively repress them. Fear of them can blind us and block our progress.

Evil doesn't seek its own reform. Neither does pure agnosticism seek to believe. Doubt and despair include the germ of faith, because each implies the wish for something more.

Jesus often said the people who knew that they were in need of God were the blessed ones who would be given faith. *Blessed are the poor in spirit*

Somehow it doesn't seem American or praiseworthy to be so passive. I want to get at the believing business aggressively. That's how I'm used to working at anything.

Oh, I don't mind if you go ahead and work at many things. Read avidly in the Christian texts and in Islam and Buddhism, too, for that matter.

A friend if mine used to say that reading in philosophy and astrophysics was helpful; he would end up confused at a higher level. Sure, go ahead and read. God gave us our brains and our spiritual hungers to fuel such effort too.

But simply remember this: Depending on God's gift of faith, instead of insisting we can cope with life on our own, takes a profound humility.

Hey. Am I being of any help to you at all?

I don't know, Baker. I 'm ready to keep on with this, at any rate.

Discussion Questions for Chapter 2

1. Why, if Newt doesn't believe, is he troubled?
2. Baker does not put much store in human reasoning as a source of faith. Would you want to use it more than Baker does?
3. What would you answer—as a believer, and as a doubter—if you were asked, "What sustains you?"
4. Baker says the company of believers—the church—is a place to put yourself, hoping to receive faith through that self-placement. How does that happen in your congregation?
5. Would you find transiency—the temporariness of worldly things—a demonic thing? or a blessing? Why?
6. In responding to Newt, Baker has a lot of negative talk, but there is some movement beyond saying arguments won't help Newt. Baker says stories are helpful. How does that square with your experience on the way to believing?

People love to tell stories of their personal experiences

We are drawn to people who let us share them with them. We are often comfortable & comforted if they have had similar experiences. We can be enlightened & directed by their "insights" and/or "conclusions" about them in re-looking at our experiences through their interpretations

3

Messed Up:
A Visit with Elsena

Elsena approaches a church timidly. Because of her background, and be-
cause of her social awkwardness, she has been put off by other churches
and by society at large. She wants help in coming to terms with herself. The
church secretary encounters her looking in on the sanctuary and peeking at
a parents and tots group one Monday morning. Hearing from the secretary,
Baker greets Elsena and invites her in for a few minutes.

(Elsena) You don't know me. I walk past this church a lot, but I never came in before.

It's a nice looking church. The people look nice, too. I was across the street one Sunday morning when the kids came out—all scrubbed and dressed up.

> (Baker) Yes, I like the people here. They're a friendly group.

I suppose they are, when they're with their own kind at least. I guess in churches it's like most places. Birds of a feather flock together.

> That is true, isn't it? But we try to include whoever comes here, not just the people of some particular feather. How can I help you?

21

Flock together. You don't serve Catholics, I suppose, or Jews or black people. Everybody needs a label. Can't be just Christian, I guess. After all, you're labeled as one kind on the sign out front, one particular denomination. Would it be possible for there to be a church for just everybody? Or do you have to be a church for just one kind of people? Maybe different people need different messages.

> We do have a message; that's true. But it's meant for everybody. In fact, part of the message is that everyone is welcome, and that we'll take them seriously, if they reciprocate. When people come, they can stay around if they like, without being forced into a mold that we make for them. A straightjacket.

> I'm interested in your question. You've done some thinking about this, I judge. Why do you ask?

I don't know. I visit churches sometimes. When my baby was born, I went to a minister who said he couldn't christen her because I lived alone, and the baby didn't have a father. Well, I mean she had a father of course, but we didn't know who it was. And both my boyfriends had gone anyway. Or I guess I should say I was gone. I'd moved back here so my grandmother could help me. She's lived here a long time, in this town.

> You say you often pass by here. So what made you stop in today?

I don't know, but it was a pretty day, and I was feeling good, not like usual. I think I need help. It's quiet in church. There's holiness there.

I've done some terrible things in my life. I don't know how to turn around. Sometimes I just cry and cry at night. I've messed up. I've ruined just about everything. No father for Jennie, no money, no real home. My grandma puts up with me, but she don't know how to raise Jennie right. I leave Jennie with her when I work. I got a job. It don't pay much, but it helps. I don't know about your religion in this church, but today I remembered those children that Sunday. What would it take to make Jennie like that?

> Make Jennie like that? I don't understand.

Well, neat and clean and happy. Jennie's three, but she isn't happy the way other kids are, it seems to me. She whimpers a lot. She's tiny. I took her to McDonald's and she didn't even enjoy that. Fuss, fuss, fuss. I can't seem to do right by Jennie.

You say you messed up?

I messed up in everything. My mom, who isn't so great herself, says I don't amount to nothing. I can't live with her anymore. It's no place for Jennie. I was sort of white trash when I lived with her. In Kentucky. I was a wild teenager. I had a lot of boyfriends, and we drank all the time, and I never finished high school. I really messed up. I still do. Came back to this town and Grandma's place for a few years, and she managed to straighten me out a little. She made me get a high school certificate—through night school while I worked at the plastic factory—they make purses you know—over there on Fourth Street.

But then I messed up again. I went to Cincinnati where a friend of mine had an apartment, and we got into a fast life. People wanted me to do drugs with them and all that. So I came here after Jennie was born—to this smaller town.

Hilda thought it was a good idea too. She was the sister at the clinic, who really just about saved my life. She'd call, or even come to the apartment, when I'd miss an appointment, to keep track of me. It sort of balanced the pressure from the guys—and the street. When someone cares about you, you've got a reason to get up in the morning.

Anyway, this is a lot better place to raise Jennie than Cincinnati is. Or Kentucky. I can't go back to Kentucky—I'd have to serve some time.

I see. We do have a good community. I hope Jennie and you get along well here.

I took Jennie to a church one time—to its Sunday school nursery. I left her there and went to the service, but I was nervous. And they had communion. People went up front, you know, and all that. I'd dressed up well enough that I thought I might almost fit in. I thought I was supposed to go up front with the other people. But they had people fill out little cards first, and I was sure then that I wasn't good enough. Maybe one day I'll be better and believe more. I sure hope I get better.

Better? In what way?

In just about every way you can name. So I'm in this place for now. It just has to be a better place for Jennie.

> That sounds pretty important. It sounds like you are sort of starting out with a new page of your life. New baby, new place for Jennie, new life without drugs, a visit to a new church. Am I seeing too much importance in the fact that you came in?

You make it sound like a big thing—but I guess it is big. Living with the guys in Cincinnati was just great sometimes when we were high, but it tore me apart too. And when I thought of Jennie growing up like—well, you know, when she was born I thought I'd die and then I thought I'd melt into nothing. I was scared and ashamed and at the same time I was determined to show the world I could make it with this helpless, little, adorable thing. She was beautiful, you know, and I couldn't stand to hurt her. Anyway, I saw right away I couldn't take that street life anymore. I need a new life, I really do.

> One of the followers of Jesus wrote about starting over. "If anyone is in Christ," he said, "he or she is made new." I like that because starting over again is what we often have to do. But every one of us needs help to turn over a new leaf. It's hard. We believe God can help us as we follow Jesus. Also, God helps us through other people.

And if you don't believe in God, where does that leave you? Or if God has decided to throw you away? Other people seem to believe right, but I can't. Why can't I just decide to start over and do it? When I was in Cincinnati I started over, I tried really hard, about ten times, I think. But I slipped back every time.

> I think I understand. The man who talked about being made new was Saint Paul. Paul also said he couldn't understand his own actions. His mind wanted to do one thing, to go one way. But he ended up doing the opposite. We all need help.

That's how it was in Cincinnati. Like drinking and AA. You tell yourself not to drink, but someone calls you a slut, or insults you some other way, or you even just pass a bar, and it's like your body does the opposite from what you're telling yourself to do. So you miss a half day of work and need money and you're on the street and going down again.

If you've been through all that you know a lot about wanting to do one thing, but ending up doing something else. That is what Christ can help you with.

I think you might want to bring Jennie to meet Sarah Swanson, our toddlers' teacher, and the other children in the Sunday school toddlers group. She's good with children. That might be a start.

That wouldn't be fair would it, with me not a member or anything? Like I say, I don't have a faith. And I don't support this place.

We can live with that, I'm sure. That's what we're here for. We don't send out bills, you know.

Your mom says you don't amount to anything, and you say you've messed up. I think you may be stronger than you realize. You had the strength to leave Cincinnati. You had the nerve to come in here today. You care deeply about Jennie. You're aware that you've done wrong things. You hope to do better.

I do. Yes, I do. Working at the plastic factory, I see the women in the office. I could do that kind of work if I had a little more education. One of the ladies there gave me a ride one time. She was learning computers then and told me about it. She has a good life—has a husband and two children and a house of her own. No relatives crowding up the place. I don't know how she got started, but I'm sure it wasn't by messing up.

Elsena, did you ever hear the story about Jesus and the woman who was caught with a man who was not her husband? There were people who wanted to punish her—they thought it was right even to kill a person for adultery in those days. And Jesus stepped in between those people and that woman and stared them down. They were going to stone her. That usually meant killing. And Jesus said, "Let the person who has not sinned at all, ever in his life, let that man throw the first stone." And nobody threw a single stone. And Jesus told her that her sins were forgiven, and he told her to go and sin no more. He saved her life. And I believe he gave her strength to straighten out her life. I think God gave her courage to try again and forget the street and the drink and the dope and gave her courage to be somebody for the sake of her friends and her children, if she had any.

I suppose that's from the Bible. Doesn't it say how it all came out?

> Only that the men went away without harming her, and that Jesus forgave her. We have a lot of things in the Bible that are left up to our imaginations.

I guess I don't understand the Bible very well.

> There is plenty in the Bible that you can understand. We spend time in our Bible study groups starting with the parts that are easier, I assure you. And we have a lot of disagreements, even then. At any rate, it's a lot easier in a group. And the groups make for some wonderful friendships. That seems to be why the people come, as much or more than the actual knowledge they receive.

I'd better go. Do you really think it would be okay for Jennie to come some Sunday morning?

> I really do. You've had hard times, Elsena. Did I get the name right? If you come early some Sunday, I'll introduce you and Jennie to Mrs. Swanson myself.

Discussion Questions for Chapter 3

1. It took courage on Elsena's part to go in to see Baker. How can we make our churches less intimidating to young people like Elsena?
2. We believe the church is part of God's intention for the world, and that it is part of what helps people toward faith. Not every congregation welcomes an unwed mother. In what ways can you imagine the church helping Elsena to develop her spiritual life? How would she get along in your congregation?
3. What is the main message in the gospel for Elsena? Is it the same message that is there for you? Does the gospel come in different tones of voice to different people?
4. If they move further into faith, in what different ways will Newt and Sophie and Elsena probably find God shaping their lives? How about you?
5. What would Elsena's life look like if she were given stronger faith? What would it mean for the people in the pews if Elsena's experience is going to be different from what it was in other churches?

4

Truth:
A Visit with Newt

Newt returns for another conversation with Baker.

(Newt) My mind has been churning since last week. We didn't get very far. I left with more questions than I came with.

(Baker) For instance?

You said mainly that I won't find belief or faith on my own. Faith is more of a gift, you said. We didn't talk much about the actual things I can't believe.

We said little about belief, but we said a good bit about Christian faith.

There's a difference?

In my book, yes. By belief I mean an intellectual framework, or summary. I need that framework so as to understand faith better. Faith is that inner disposition of my whole person, my whole self, toward God. Of course, faith and belief interact. Each can shape the other to an extent. I admit that not everyone uses the words the same way.

I didn't leave you altogether hopeless last week, did I?

In making some kind of faith for myself? Almost. You said I couldn't do much. I could mix with Christians, but that's about all. That's not exactly twelve steps on "how to believe"!

No. But that's my point. It's a temptation to think we can cobble together a formula of belief that will save us.

But haven't people done that throughout history?

They've tried. But once we think we can build a faith system from our own human resources, we lose God. We center on human agency. Spiritual technique or mental wizardry displaces Godward amazement. And amazement is where faith begins.

But we build the cathedrals. Or should we say that religion is something we humans create, different from faith? And faith is the gift?

That wouldn't be a bad way of putting it. Faith involves awe and gratitude. The cathedrals and religious language and liturgy are what we do to express that. That response does involve human agency, of course.

However, I may have lost you already. You probably don't have much interest in theological hairsplitting and might not even if you came in from outside the circle of theological language. One need not talk theology in order to believe.

I don't follow you. What is it you mean by saying I am outside? Aren't you making the church into an elitist secret society, like a club with special regulations, esoteric language, and innovative handshakes? I'm really turned off by that.

No, far from it. In fact, my church is rife with outsiders. We are often accused of being too wide open and of lacking enough regulation and code and ritual. We have fewer overt behavioral requirements than a civic club. In fact, we are all outsiders in part.

When I say "outsider," I don't mean to put you down or push you away. Scratch that word "outside" from the record. I'm simply recognizing that language is a social product. It acquires meaning within a community. Communal life rests on commonly held assumptions about reality. In this matter your language world simply doesn't assume God's reality the way ours does.

Does "assuming God," as you put it, make so much difference? I don't think it blocks communication as much as you make it sound. You and I are talking across the difference, at any rate.

But I'm being careful to use the language that works on the outside. What if I said "Jesus died for your sins"? Wouldn't you say that is nonsense? Jesus died long ago.

Yes, I probably would.

And yet that assertion means a lot to most people in the pews.

Give me another example, another case where language points to more than my assumptions can take in. I want to find out whether I'm as far outside as you think I am.

A trivial example then—easier at least than "Jesus died for my sins." Let's say the outsider hears that Jesus was born in Bethlehem, and then reads a critical historical account that says Jesus was probably born a good way north of Judea, in Nazareth, of Galilee. The outsider's conclusion? Either that the Christmas stories ought to be changed in keeping with historical research, or if Christians keep the stories, they are following a myth instead of truth. That's outsider thinking.

I agree. What you call outsider thinking makes sense to me. You could almost be quoting me. What alternative can there be?

For a person on the inside, there is a rich set of meanings in the story as it is, set in the city of David, reporting on "wise men" from the East, describing shepherds and angels, speaking of a housing shortage that night, and a birth out back in a barn. Then Matthew adds that coda about Herod's atrocity paralleling Pharaoh's slaughter of the infants—the one Moses escaped— and about fleeing to and coming "out of" Egypt. The meanings derive from an entire tradition of prophecy and narrative— quasihistorical lore and psalmody with which the genuine outsider can scarcely identify. That tradition embodies truths of which geography and petty history know little. And it all has to do with the story of God redeeming the world. It has to do with the world's preoccupation with other matters, its resistance to holy things. It has to do with God's gracious self-giving in weakness and vulnerability, rather than in power.

I guess I am a real outsider. You said last time you want me to keep my integrity. My integrity makes me prefer Nazareth as the birthplace, not Bethlehem. It wants clarity, not mumbo jumbo. It wants the truth.

I sympathize. Jesus was born in Nazareth, taught in Galilee and Judea, and was executed. There you have the facts about Jesus of Nazareth. But I'm not satisfied we have there the truth of Jesus. Religious truth is a far more dynamic concept than material facticity. Jesus, in John's Gospel, tells Thomas, the doubter, "I am the way, the truth, and the life." That usage transforms the meaning of "truth," if we can catch on to it. Truth is changed from a dead accumulation of information into a claim on one's loyalty. Such a claim is part of truth, isn't it?

You're saying truth goes deeper than fact. But we begin with the facts, surely.

Facts are arm's length kinds of things; truth, religiously understood at least, is for the soul. Truth goes deeper. It is a fact that Jesus was executed. To us it is religious truth that he was crucified and that the crucifixion changes the world.

You are losing me now. Where would you put the gospels in a collection of book reviews? Would it come under fiction? or nonfiction?

I never thought of truth as telling a story. A story can illustrate truth, of course. But truth is something to be asserted, described, defended.

Could we propose, perhaps, that there are two kinds of truth, one more like your engineering textbooks, another more philosophical, less precise? The latter could include what I am calling deeper truth.

The first one would include tangible fact. The scientific truths, for example, that feed our fascination with how things work. The other kind might be called poetic truth. Whatever we call it, it takes in the world of meaning, emotion, moral values, personal virtues, and the arts, like music.

That might help me.

All right. The time was when truth was almost entirely of the second kind. The primitives knew something about natural process, of course, but everything also had its spirit dimension, its enchantment. Nothing was merely machine. All reality was seen through eyes keyed in on mystery. The world was structured by a liturgical vision, through religious narrative and poetic sensibility.

Interesting. And now, with such pervasive scientific awareness, that's been reversed. We finally know what's going on—in scientific terms. And you think that's bad for us?

> No. We profit immensely from our science, of course, but we're out of balance. The de-sacralizing of the world comes with immense costs. We probably now need less the prose of science than we need the poetry of depth and meaning. Without that we lose the truth. Reality and truth not only come measured. They come sung and danced. They come lived out in committed loyalties and holy fidelity.

Let me try to describe my reaction. Maybe I'm hung up on science. But I'm not sure you take me seriously. You're right. Reality does mainly seem to me to consist of these harder facts, the ones measured.

> Surely the nonmeasured has a claim to be called real. And we can debate statements about it as true or false.

> Tell me more about your reality; it seems terribly limited to me. Maybe you could provide me an example.

Well, take the genetic code. That is a reality. It's not the product of human imagination alone, although a lot of imagination went into our work on it. Anybody in a good laboratory anywhere in the world will reach the same results from the same experiment.

In the softer sciences, like psychology, or political science, or in the arts, your so-called "truth" is a matter of opinion. There's no set answer. Truth, if you can use the word at all, is terribly blurred. There's no single definition of beauty, for instance. It's all according to the subjective mindset of the observer.

> Agreed that there's a lot more subjectivity involved in the non-scientific realm. That, to me, is part of its charm. And its importance. Science misses that dimension—by its own intention. By making its own rules that try hard to avoid the personal and the subjective.

> But would you really want to say that dream life and baroque artistic style and socialism and generosity are unreal? Those

things can have immense cultural impact. I suppose they all have their material location, for that matter. (Apparently, each memory and thought process has material analogue, minute as it may be—a wrinkle or electronic field or something in the brain.) But physiological language about molecules and neurons doesn't say the truth about these things as well as the larger words do. Or the way, in religion, that stories do.

But I'm wandering far afield. I understand you, I think. You say you can't believe because in religious talk you can't find the same kind of experimental certainty or measurable reliability that you find in science. And I say there's too much richness to reality to flatten it out and limit it to the measurable.

Yes. I'm not much of a poet. Poetic truth always seems too nebulous or derivative to me, coming after the hard facts. Is there really any other option?

Of course. For example, there's one philosophical tradition arguing that mind and/or spirit is the firmer reality, and that all material, sensate experience is the derivative side of things, less real. Some have even put all this in moral terms—spirit things are good, and the material things are bad or evil, per se.

To my mind other religions are more likely to go that way than Christianity. Christianity—with its creation stories and its interest in material history and its doctrine of incarnation—is willingly materialistic. We affirm the palpable world. God, we say, intended it and called it good.

So you're saying I could keep my science and believe, as well?

Of course. Christians celebrate both scientific knowledge and poetic truth, in our special meaning of "poetic."

And actually both are human responses to the universe that's given us. They are two aspects of the same world. That just might help solve the problem of science and religion. The world has to be one, but its parts break apart so easily.

Remember that beyond all our little pictures of what is real, there is the ultimate mystery—that this universe exists, for example, rather than not existing. With that there are joy and music and beauty—and chemistry and biology. But the first are so much more than mere brain function or audio mechanics or measurable line, form, and weight.

We're not calling religion mere poetry, I hope. Belief must be more than aesthetics. Even from my place outside your theological talk, I would object to such a proposal.

You still want more certainty, I think?

Exactly. Who can live without some kind of foundation to depend upon? That's the appeal of science and the materialist view. We prove our conclusions in science.

And they don't change?

Well, no. I can't say that. New theories are always coming up. New facts even change old ones. And the so-called physical world, when you get down to it, evaporates into a kind of empty space full of energy and fields and waves. On the grand scale, cosmic space is beyond comprehension, too, with its dark matter, its black holes, and its sheer immensity.

Ultimate certainty may be almost as elusive for the scientist as for the poet, then?

I wouldn't say that. But we need to guard against being dogmatic. We need to remember Galileo and Copernicus—who so radically changed the previous certainties in science. Changed them against the will of the religious leadership of their time, too, I might remind you. We need to keep science experimental and flexible, as new perspectives come along.

Yes. Humility is far more attractive than magisterial certainty in any field.

The assumptive world of anyone is a kind of faith. Even in science, an initial faith guides your energies. You choose what kind of investigation you will do and why. And you start with axioms taken somewhat on faith, although you may want to argue that point. You assume the universality of nature's law, for example, and a cause-effect sequence in time.

But I still persist; gift though it be, can't we still ask how religious faith comes about?

> I think the change of assumptive worlds is like the way an optical illusion shifts. What seemed implausible or invisible suddenly makes more sense or becomes visible. What was resisted is now your choice. You move to a new vantage point, a new perspective.

As with the Copernican revolution, I think.

> Yes, but in a religious shift we ask immense change in people. Jesus comes into the disciples' lives saying, "Follow me," and on the spot they leave their work to do just that. He says to one, "Go and sin no more"; to another whose life is also changing through healing, "Your sins are forgiven. Take up your bed and go home."

> He tells us to mimic the heavenly pattern of sending rain and sun to both the evil and the good, loving our enemies, becoming like servants or slaves for the good of others. Getting our own pride and avarice out of the way in deference to the neighbor's well-being goes against the human grain, but that is the shift in outlook. That is the Christian's Copernican revolution.

I wish I could believe that way.

> One more word. Then we must close. This shift may come suddenly, as it does in the optical illusion experience. But not necessarily.

If it comes to me, it will come very slowly, I'm sure.

Discussion Questions for Chapter 4

1. Baker offends Newt by calling him an outsider to Christian talk. In what ways is our church language in danger of alienating the very people we want to help?
2. How does Baker's view on the birth stories (Luke on the shepherds, Matthew with his wise men) affect the way you hear the Christmas stories?
3. Newt says the first interview didn't help much, but it urged him to "mix with Christians." What particular people and/or programs of your parish might be of help to Newt in his search for faith?
4. Baker says "Amazement is where faith begins." Some other candidates for that role of prompting faith are moral struggle, the need for

communal support, logic or speculative reason, loyalty to Jesus, or even guilt. Where would you say it begins for you? How do you think religion arose historically?

5. How would you answer Newt's question about the classification of the gospels—fiction or nonfiction?

6. Newt proposes scientific and philosophical as two types of language about reality, the second being "less precise," he says. Baker proposes prose and poetry. What other words could be used to express what they are each getting at? Are there truths that can only be "sung and danced"?

7. Baker calls Christianity "willingly materialistic." What would that imply about our Christian interest in science, or economic problems, or craftsmanship? How does it affect the idea that the real quest in religion is for spiritual peace of mind?

8. Newt thinks his own "optical illusion" experience—conversion—will take place gradually, if at all. How would you anticipate your conversion, if it is to be in the future, or how did you experience it in the past? How can this be reconciled with the previous comments of these two about the persistence of doubt? Does this analogy imply that a reverse conversion can also take place, the world thereafter being seen through a lens of skepticism and despair?

5

Law:
A Visit with Linda

Baker meets Linda in the public library where Linda works and invites her to stop in at the church for a chat. Puzzled, Linda comes by shortly thereafter.

(Baker) I'm concerned about you, Linda. We've missed you. The divorce was almost a year ago. Your friends say you haven't been out much, even in town. You used to be so active.

(Linda) I suppose they're right. I have kept to myself. In fact I've been lonely. My knee-jerk reaction to your comment was almost, "What friends?" But I held my peace.

I think I'm getting along all right; I don't expect people to welcome me with open arms after all this. It isn't like breaking your arm and then wearing a cast for a month. People can ask you about your arm.

I don't follow you. You mean you don't talk to people about your divorce?

Of course not. You don't parade your sins in public, especially in this town. People talk enough as it is. But I appreciate your concern.

We do miss you. And I'm sure the choir does, especially.

It's much too early to think about singing again. The choir is a pretty close-knit group. Divorce seems to create a lot of collateral damage. Breaking the big relationship breaks the little ones too. I'm not ready to cope with that one yet.

> You mean to cope with those relationships? Have people implied that they don't want you around or something?

No. But I know when I've broken the rules. I can't pretend to rate a seat in the choir.

> "Rate"? I don't understand.

I think of the choir as a special place—up front that way. And I've had a divorce. That rules me out, in my book. It would be like an illegal immigrant trying to vote.

> You feel disqualified? But to me, your voice sounds as strong and well-tuned as ever.

My voice is fine. My virtue is not.

> Harold said once that you were a perfectionist. But we'd been talking about the choir. So I thought then he was talking about the singing, not the virtue, whatever you mean by that.

Yes, Harold accused me of perfectionism more than once. He usually did it when I had asked him to pick up his tools after finishing some little project around the house. Our guests would go past his shop on the way to the back yard. He usually closed the door, and he argued that was enough. But there's nothing like a workroom that's all neat and orderly to complete the impression of a well-kept house.

Well, you don't want sloppy musicians in a symphony. And you don't want divorcees in a church choir.

> And you can't have imperfect people in the community of saints?

Right. If there's one thing clear in the Bible, it's that God gives us a law to live by. Our civilization is built on the Ten Commandments. That's what I try to teach my kids. And so far they have been toeing the line. I'm very proud of them. That's about all I can be proud of right now.

The divorce has been hell. (Excuse the French.) It's been very difficult.

I don't know how it happened. In that strange note he left me, Harold said that he had lived more than half his life, and he wanted to dance some more before it was all over. I don't know what he meant. He knows I'm a morally serious person. And I had always thought he was too.

Harold was more and more casual about a lot of things. He'd drive above the speed limit. He'd give away money on the street to worthless people. When things came up that he wanted to do, he'd cancel appointments that he had made in all seriousness. Once in a while he'd drink too much.

> These were serious flaws?

Don't you think so? Being a good Christian doesn't exactly require that a person be picky about good manners, I suppose. But we do have to live within the law. I try to remember that the Ten Commandments are like a centerpiece in the Bible.

> You have an unusual religious emphasis—for these times, at least—on the law. You may have told me before, so forgive me if you did, but what was your religious background, Linda?

Oh, I came from a very religious home. Christian was our middle name. We prayed regularly. And we talked about the rules. Religion was an everyday matter, not just Sunday. It guided us in everything—what we could do in our free time, how we should relate to different kinds of people, to grandparents, to people of the opposite sex, to nonbelievers.

I started to rebel against all that once, when I met people who were supposed to be Christians but rationalized their loose behavior with theories of relativism. That seemed to me the way that leads to destruction—for them, for me, and for our country. So I came back to Christianity and found my home. I try to help people learn the laws of God—about personal faith and about public behavior.

People don't give these matters enough thought. As someone put it, Moses didn't bring down from Sinai two tablets with ten suggestions on them. They were commandments.

"Theories of relativism"? I'm not sure I know what you mean.

It came first with kids who were my peers in high school. They lied to me and didn't realize they were doing wrong. These were kids who rationalized their falsehoods or their petty thefts. Then I saw it in the teenagers who took sexual mores only casually. One of my friends got pregnant. Another got AIDS, a homosexual, it turned out. I started a club. We called it The Hundred Percent Club—meaning we would obey the religious law a hundred percent. We had other names before that one, which finally stuck. We started off as the Second Milers, and then the "'I'-dotters." We are still close, although we dispersed when we grew up and went off to school and got married and all that. Now we live clear across the country. We hope we're contributing to the renewal of our communities and our country, in our own little way. Some have fallen by the way, of course. And I'm not sure what my relation will be now, of course, myself.

> That's quite a story. No wonder your divorce is so upsetting. Have you been recovering at all—from the trauma of the divorce? It must have caught you terribly off guard.

Recovering? I don't seem to be. There's no way to change God's law. We humans don't make the law—that would be reversing the right order of things. It would be like the tower of Babel—concocting our own norms. The judgment is yet to come for us. It would be like Adam and Eve without God's punishment. It would be great for me if things were different, but this is just something I have to live with. My cross to bear. That's what I have to learn.

> You do indeed. You can't erase facts—events that have happened. But you don't have to live with it the way you say, Linda. The Bible—in the Old and New Testaments alike—emphasizes forgiveness as much as it does the law, which you have focused on.

People have to pay for their sin.

> You describe a very sober life, Linda. Doesn't God ever smile for you?

Does God ever smile? Of course, when we please him, I guess he smiles. But God isn't whimsical. The relativists make God unreliable. They talk about forgiveness *ad nauseam*.

I think I'm talking about something else. Your viewpoint hems life in too much, it seems to me. Maybe smile isn't the right word. Does God ever give you freedom to do things for which there are not any guidelines all spelled out ahead of time? Does God ever say, as one of the saints put it, "So long as you love your neighbor, do as you please?" Does God ever say, "Go ahead. Be creative. I won't dominate your every minute"? Does God ever say, "Tell me some jokes"? Does God tell jokes?

I wouldn't think so. Faith is very serious business. It has to do with the world's salvation, and that depends on our doing right or our doing wrong. Surely you agree with that.

Actually, Linda, I don't. In fact, I don't think you believe in the God we announce after the confession every Sunday. You remember you said the Ten Commandments are the centerpiece of the Bible? I take exception. Mercy and forgiveness are the core of the gospel, not the commandments. Human repentance is part of that transaction, of course. But that God we meet in Jesus is a God of assurance, a God of mercy.

It isn't just Jesus, of course. Hosea, in the Hebrew scriptures, married a prostitute and said that it was a sign that God cared about Israel even when Israel sinned. The psalmist said God forgives all our iniquities. I don't hear much forgiveness in your God, Linda. Jesus said the blessed people, the happy people were those who made peace and sought the kingdom and were meek, and merciful; not only those who obeyed the law.

And he said the pure in heart. And those who hunger and thirst for righteousness. And the ones persecuted for righteousness' sake.

Yes, both emphases are important.

What in the world is the purpose of the law if it isn't meant to be obeyed?

I would say it's a gift of God's graciousness—to guide us, to teach us how to live. But we can't live, you know, without the forgiveness. What would you say?

I try not to need forgiveness. I try to live out the law. But I guess I need forgiveness now, if I'm going to get over this divorce thing. Something in it must have been my fault. Sometimes I think there is no recovery now at all. I did sin, somehow, even if I couldn't begin to explain what happened. Harold just left; that's the fact.

But God isn't giving us the easy life. He's laying down the law. Listen to the prophets. They're angry. They talk about God's rage at the way people treat each other—we human beings torture each other, we abuse children, kill and maim in war. God is utterly serious and justified in his anger; he wants obedience.

> You know that song, "Amazing Grace"? You ought to sing that song at least once a day.

I know the song, but I don't especially care for it. It's terribly sentimental.

Baker, why can't I believe in that forgiving God and move on with my life, the way most people seem to?

> That's probably a pretty deep question that will take some time to fathom. I'm sure we are part of the problem, Linda—we in the church. In our pride, in the false fronts we put up, we almost pretend we're a club of the sinless angels instead of a clinic for sinners. I guess we fail to give people a powerful and persuasive picture of the forgiving side of God.

> In that song it says, a "wretch like me." I thought that was what you were going to say you didn't like. That's where some people react. But we're all in it together, as Saint Paul says. "All have fallen short." I survive by being forgiven, time and time again. I live by grace.

Do you not live by law?

> I don't think that can be done, not fully. I try, of course. But that's the wrong starting point; it's not the central emphasis.

It's where the Bible starts, isn't it? The first thing God told Adam and Eve was about the tree they couldn't eat from.

> Before the rules, the Bible starts with this amazing creativity of God—an entire universe—for God's enjoyment and for human enjoyment. And the creation was good. That's the first word, the first sign of grace.

> The limits are there, yes. But first there is that overwhelming generosity of the creation—that God bothered to make it at all. That's where I see the starting point.

I don't think I ever thought of it that way. It's a very different place to begin to read, isn't it?

> Your emphasis on the law is real enough. But Saint Paul said the law, of itself, was dead. It needs its complement—God's grace. Otherwise we're all condemned. Moralism is a dead-end street, if you're at all sensitive to moral issues. Once the wrong has been committed, where do you go next? The more moral you are, the worse it gets. And you're one who's sensitive like that. Even if we could complete every positive action to perfection, we'd still have to deal with all the vast sins of omission that stand beyond what we can imagine. Moralism can't deal with that. It can only condemn us.

> Linda, our responsible, steady, daily work of obedience is mighty important. But so, too, is the grace.

I thought you were going to say, "so, too, is the dancing."

> You sing, Linda. Do you dance?

I wish I had learned to dance with Harold. How desperately I wish that.

It's hard to change. Harold wasn't a bad husband. And I thought I was a good wife.

Do you think that's all Harold meant about dancing? That he couldn't abide my strictness?

> It may have meant a lot of things.

Harold was easygoing. He didn't see things the way I do. He allowed people their faults without criticizing them, and it gave me the creeps. He'd eat fatty foods and ride with smokers and, on the first Thursday of every last month, he'd go out to play poker and gamble—just for small stakes. I always disliked the evenings when it was his turn to entertain them. They were so macho then. So full of themselves. I ended up going out to movies.

> But God loves those buddies, too, don't you see? Or do you believe that?

> Once we see their faults, we lose our buddies—our friends—unless we know about the grace in life as well as the law.

In theory, yes. I hear that from Jesus, that God loves everybody. But that seems too cheap. I want a strenuous religion. Why can't I measure up?

> Why can't any of us? But measuring up isn't where faith begins. It begins with awe. I start the day saying "Praise God," not, "Obey God." Obedience—what I can muster—comes only second, at the earliest. And put there, I think it actually comes more easily than if I started with it.

I wish I could believe all that.

> Linda, you can. You know now that you are far from perfect, if you never knew it before. As am I. All human beings sin and fail and fall. What do you think the passion story is all about? We are distant from God, in need of God's initiative to heal and accept us. But that initiative has come. That's what Christians mean by the cross. Let go. Enjoy these people around you here. And let up in your judgment of them. It's playing God in a way, and you know the dangers in that. The very first commandment warns about displacing God. Let God do the judging.
>
> I was serious about "Amazing Grace." Sing it out every day for a month in that good voice of yours, whether you come back to the choir or not. I dare you to do that. You'll be in my prayers. I think you've been terribly misled in what you think Christianity is all about.

You give me more to think about—and feel about—than I can take in. Just keeping up my self-respect takes most of my energy. Changing who God is changes who I am, and having lived as me for thirty years, changing it all around would be like learning to lead a different life, like being a child again, or like a new birth.

> I can see that. It will be a struggle. One more suggestion then, and I'll stop. List the experiences in your life when you've received something as a gift, rather than having earned it. Work hard on that. It should be a long list.
>
> There's another side to faith besides justice and fairness and obedience. A wild unruly side of things. And in it somewhere is God, being extravagant with divine mercy.

You've given me quite a lecture, Baker. That isn't like you. A lot of food for thought.

I feel like a naughty child, but even so your words are more generous than my father's reprimands. I'm so confused so much of the time. And I need something to hold on to. Something to be certain of.

Discussion Questions for Chapter 5

1. Linda said that the Ten Commandments were the centerpiece of the Bible. What would you say is the center?

2. Can a person believe partially? What does Baker mean when he says that Linda doesn't "believe in the God we announce in the words of assurance after the confession every Sunday"?

3. Linda is worried about what she calls cheap religion. How important is her desire for a strenuous faith?

4. How does a serious moralist come to believe in forgiveness deeply enough that it will lift the weight of the past? Doesn't easy forgiveness trivialize the law? Doesn't it undermine the biblical idea of righteousness? Linda fears it will lead to a lax, morally loose society. What do you think?

5. Someone has said that people of our time no longer feel that guilt separates them from God. What does alienate them from God and spiritual well-being, they say, is shame, the feeling that they are not right inside, not acceptable by the community, so much that they want to cover up and hide. Based on your experience, how would you respond to such an argument?

6

Scripture and Dogma: A Visit with Newt

Newt continues his inquiry.

(Newt) I have wondered for a long time about this. You Christians seem to ascribe a mysterious authority to the Bible, as if God in heaven had dictated the text.

> (Baker) Authority, yes. But only a small, literalist fraction of Christians hold to divine dictation.
>
> I don't think the authority matter is so strange, when you think of the role of the Constitution in our national life or the respect claimed by the Declaration of Independence.

Granted. But is the Bible any more distinctive than Shakespeare or the Magna Carta? You all imply that it is, the way you talk.

> It's not magic. It was written by mortals. But the Bible does play a special role for Christians. It focuses more consistently on the God relation than other literature, and it's full of the assumption that God acts through particular people and events in our Jewish and Christian history. It arises from a long history of holy encounter.

But that's not what you're asking, I think.

No. Calling it "God's word" is what troubles me. As if these were not humanly written documents, reporting on real people—Moses, or the prophets, or Jesus? The Bible is full of human foibles, human culture, and human errors. Besides, the Bible has some terrible things in it, like hoping that the heads of enemy children are dashed against the rocks.

> Yes, the Bible is probably more genuinely human and grainy than the bulk of what passes as spiritual literature these days. But the metaphor about God's word isn't so surprising, is it? Not if people have found spiritual power in texts they know and love. Spiritual insight is rare enough.

But is it any different from other holy books, do you think? Aren't the same kinds of things in all of them?

> Yes, but from what little I know comparatively, each has a particular style to it, too, deriving from its own culture. There are relationships among them of course. Muslims call us Jews and Christians "people of the book," like themselves. We all share the heritage of Abraham, Moses, Elijah, and the prophets. And with Muslims, we Christians share the stories of Jesus and Mary.

You portray in this holy Bible a God who is not so holy, I think. God has all manner of human attributes—anger and jealousy and vengefulness.

> And mercy and magnanimity and forgiveness and compassion and love and steadfastness and wisdom and power. The Muslims go on for ninety-nine names.

> But let's stay on track. We're talking about the Bible.

> Scripture comprises a community's legends, myths, and testimonies—cherished because they are essential to its identity. Since we in the church believe God called us into faith, we see divine self-disclosure in the scriptures. They're a gift, like faith itself.

But why give the Bible all this authority, when it's so mixed in quality?

> I'm not doing well in explaining, am I? Looking at it from inside, the Bible does several things for us. In a way, it tells us who

we are. It binds us together across all kinds of differences and across centuries as well. It roots us in the past. When we disagree, we're charged to check our thinking against biblical perspectives, and this often helps us understand one another. The Bible offers guidance and moral law. It provides much of our language of devotion and liturgy. It's a voice from "outside," a plumb line for common reference among the diverse arguments that head off in so many different (and often circular) patterns of thought.

By providing us our language and so much of our religious lore this way, it gives us an identity as a people of God. Deep and subtle assumptions and allusions are built into a language and cannot be exchanged casually for some other document.

Again, as with faith itself, you may have to live with us awhile before this makes sense.

Then you can reverence the Bible as you do in spite of its historical errors and its brutality?

Yes. The sublime outweighs the brutal overwhelmingly. Think of the Psalms, Job, and the parables and Ruth, Hosea, or the gospels. It's the whole central story that catches us up in faith, not the piecemeal texts.

I agree that the narrative sections are often very rich. Anyone can see that. I think of the Genesis saga from the garden all the way through the patriarchs and the Joseph epic and the escape from Egypt. I like it better than the *Odyssey*. And the long David story in Kings and Samuel.

And the prophets—parts of Isaiah and Jeremiah—powerful.

But what about the Canaanites, the victims of this "chosen people"? Shouldn't they have a say?

They were shortchanged, by our standards, weren't they? I can't change that. But note that your compulsion for siding with victims of avarice or oppression probably comes from these same scriptures.

Agreed, although I might have worried about them even without a personal experience with your holy writ. And the errors? Why not correct them?

Hamlet is full of "errors" if you try to make it history. History simply is not Hamlet's function. Hamlet probes deeper matters of the human spirit.

The biblical editors and writers were not doing historical research in the modern way. They had other purposes in mind. And different lyricists sing different ballads, or similar songs, but with different accents. The four gospels offer textures of faith with nuanced variety.

When you call all this God's word or God's gift, I guess you are on the poet side, but I follow you. As I see it, you're telling me two things. I can start reading the Bible without turning off my critical bent. And I needn't fret about the details if I can catch the larger purposes of the writers.

Right.

Maybe this discussion of the Bible can lead into my other question for today.

Which is?

I can understand the variety in scripture, but what is the point of all the dogma that so divides people? Wouldn't we be better off without it? In the name of religious doctrine, secular and spiritual tyrants have caused untold human suffering. People have invented enemies, waged war, burned "witches."

Faith has to be more than a good feeling on sunny spring days. Human commitments in dedicated "faith"—and I mean to put that in quotation marks—could come in any number of bizarre shapes. It makes a difference how we define the ultimate ground of things. Is God a great watchmaker who sets the cosmic machinery going, and the moral law, and then stands back as a spectator? Or is God an agent of growth and development, involved, for example, in the rise and fall of nations? Does God really address us through ancient prophets and seers and through Jesus? How about other pivotal figures like Buddha and Socrates? And when these voices disagree, which one is better? Do I simply follow private hunches born of my "faith"?

So dogma tries to answer questions like that?

Exactly. Every faith group, if it starts to think, has to work on questions like that. As the theologians say, faith seeks understanding. And, because it's so easy for a lone person to be wrong and self-deceived, the community is important. Doctrine comes from the community.

But doesn't that make faith into what you call belief all over again—the emphasis on doctrine?

Certainly many fear just that, so they avoid dogma and doctrine like the plague. The noncreedal churches have a noble tradition behind them, born of that fear. But no, that fear is a misunderstanding that arises when the creeds turn rigid.

Theology arises from the experience we have of God, past and present. If it loses touch with experience, we have to leave it aside for a while. Jesus often contested ancient convictions and habits when they had lost their meaning.

Nonetheless, faith wants to understand our religious experience, and there is an intellectual love of God that finds rich spiritual nurture in that effort. You've seen empty-headed piety that lacks this, I am sure. Then, too, although this has often been taken much too far and turned brittle or inhospitable and oppressive, a church needs some definition of itself in order to function well.

So I have to become at least an amateur theologian to be a Christian?

Not at all. It's rare that a person enters faith through that reflective door. Communal worship is a far more common way. Prayer is another. So, too, are other experiences—both tragic and treasured—of human death and human life.

Dogma isn't meant to convert us by philosophical argument?

There are far better ways to communicate the faith to others. We've talked about stories. A lawyer asked Jesus straight out who was his neighbor. Jesus wouldn't provide a definition. Jesus said, "A certain man went down from Jerusalem to Jericho and fell among thieves." He told a story, a parable.

Living out the stories in a community that knows them is better for conversion than dogma.

"Living them out"? Don't you mean, "Pretending they're true"?

> If you like. At moments of great doubt, that's one way to test a path that may offer hope. If I'm lost, I go a little way on one of the possible routes as if that might be the right way home.

How long will it take for my pretending to change into faith?

> God knows, and no one else. How long does it take to learn a new language? Troublesome as it may be to you, you might even have a gift of perennial doubt, a gift that may help keep others more honest, less sentimental—in the bad sense of that word. On the other hand, you may be a "quick study" who only needs a moment to turn from being a mere spectator to becoming an active Christian.

So you defend dogma, but you make it a servant rather than a master.

> That's a good way to put it, so long as you remember the norm-setting function of dogma.

Would that mean that we could change doctrine because of a change in science or culture?

Take one that seems wrong to me; I think, for example, of "original sin." That says that what a mythical figure named Adam did about a piece of fruit condemned the whole race to perdition. Adam had nothing to do with my virtue!

> You may be surprised that I would keep that in our tradition. In spite of its bad reputation, original sin sums up something we have come to know about ourselves. Every last one of us is prone to exaggerated self-interest that erodes the love of our neighbors and our judgment of what is just. Forget the biological way it was put once; the facts about human nature are there. Original sin as a teaching is a foundation for our perspectives on everything from political philosophy to the church's sacraments. It says, in short, that we all need God.

For rounding out our lives, perhaps. But not for saving me from something Adam did.

> We may have to differ on this, at least for the time being. Christian language expresses the connectedness of the human race

in ways modern society sees but poorly. We are all part of one rhizome, a single underground root. We identify with the slave as well as the slave owner of past centuries. Or the Holocaust. We of this generation "didn't do it," as people say, but we take it to heart and grieve because we know the evil side of the past and of our present. We need God to make it right; we need to be reconciled, taking evil to heart rather than dismissing it out of hand by pleading innocence for ourselves.

I don't follow you yet, but you whet my appetite for that kind of insider reflection. I think you've switched into insider talk now, way beyond the outsider's public theology.

Another dogmatic assertion that stumps me is the one about the divinity of Christ. Help me out on that. Do you think Jesus was a superman, not of our race, or was he one of us?

That is a huge question, and we'll have to work on it again. For the moment let us say two things only: The whole happening that focuses on the life of this man Jesus was part of an entire history. And it was a history through which Christians believe they have found God, or even better, God has reached out to them.

God, we say, not only reveals truth about human life and the cosmos, but also enters a powerfully saving relationship with us. That relationship is so crucial that people sought out metaphors to express it. Jesus was called the new Adam, Messiah, Prince of Peace, sacrificial lamb, God's truest Son. And yes, like other saving figures in the religions of the time, he was set into a status other than ours; he was called divine.

Second, however, the church insisted he was fully human. One text, for example, says he knew sin as we do. Divine he may have been, but the suffering of this messiah was not playacting.

I know we have to stop. But I look forward to more.

Discussion Questions for Chapter 6

1. Baker speaks of the functions served by the Bible in the faith community, primarily its provision of the "language" of the church. It also serves as an arbiter in disputes, as a devotional and liturgical resource, and as a guide for living. Would you want to introduce other functions the Bible serves?

2. Is Newt moving along with Baker, or is he holding back? He doesn't admit to seeing the Bible as specially inspired. How important is the Bible in your congregation's life and in your faith?

3. Would Newt's questioning help or hurt the learning process in your congregation's study groups?

4. Would you call your church a doctrine-based congregation? a Bible-based congregation? Where do you get the norms for your believing, for spelling out the implications of your faith?

5. How do you feel about traditional doctrines like original sin, the divinity of Christ, and the salvation wrought by the cross?

7

Kindness:
A Visit with Elsena

Elsena comes back after a month, and, seeing no secretary, tiptoes in a little sheepishly and reintroduces herself. Baker asks how she is getting on.

(Elsena) I've kept my job so far. And for me, that's going some. I missed work only one Monday morning this month, when I had a hangover. But I only got a warning slip. I've found kind of a friend at work, and that helps a lot. She's a strange lady; but she goes to AA, and she took me along. I haven't drunk so much since then. That was three weeks ago. And it helps me be more patient with Grandma. I yell at her less. And with Jennie.

(Baker) And how is Jennie?

She's pretty good. Had a little cold two weeks ago.

Oh, I bet you didn't know. I dressed her up one Sunday morning and she went to Sunday school.

Did you? Where did you go?

Right here. We slipped in and out, and no one noticed us.

That's not the way our system is supposed to work. Do I need to scold Mrs. Swanson?

Oh, I told the people not to tell anyone I was here. I don't want to get involved.

Well, I'm glad you came. Do come again, if Jennie got along all right. Do you mean you were in church, and I missed you?

No. I stayed in the nursery to help Jennie. She doesn't like new places.

Natural enough.

Mrs. Swanson read the children a story about *Alexander and the Terrible, Horrible, No Good, Very Bad Day*—I think that was the name. Jennie didn't listen much, but I loved it.

I think maybe I should read to Jennie some. But Grandma doesn't buy books.

Jennie doesn't understand about reading yet, but I think it would be good anyway.

Some people read to infants only a year old. Some even read out loud while the baby is still in the womb.

That sounds kind of silly.

I think reading is very important for children. You ought to read at least when you put Jennie down for the night, when you talk over the day and have bedtime prayers. It's a way to make the nighttime even more special for Jennie. Maybe if you did read more, your grandmother would get the idea and do more reading to Jennie herself.

Mrs. Swanson could get you a book or two to start with—from the church library. And she could tell you how to get a library card at the public library down the street, if you're going to be in this town for a while.

Would she really? She's just a volunteer on Sunday, isn't she?

Mrs. Swanson is a person who wouldn't dream of rationing out her helpfulness. She's one of those saints who is a Christian every day of the week.

What did you like about the story of Alexander?

Well, it was about Jennie's kind of day, and mine. You know, when everything goes wrong? Most days are like that.

Are there any places I could get some children's books cheap? Maybe used?

> There's a thrift store downtown here—on Gayette Street. But the library will help you without cost, if you return the books on time. (There's a real strict lady in the children's wing, I hear.) Or have Mrs. Swanson show you how to check out books from the church library. The church library doesn't have many kindergarten books yet, far from what there is at the public library.

Even if I'm not a member? That would be nice.

Well, it was nice to see you again. I'll be going.

Could you tell me something?

> I can try.

You've been nice to me. And Mrs. Swanson has. It even looks like the other people who were around last Sunday would be the same way. No one yelled at their kids. No one looked funny at me even though I was a stranger. Some of them even said, "Hello" like it was okay I was here, or even like I belonged.

Why are the people so nice? Where does that come from? I don't see what's in it for them. Do you think it's fake? Or were people all taught that way?

> I guess most of us were taught that way. But not everyone. Most go on day by day very much aware that God has been good to them and that they want to be good to other people because of that.

> And some—this is a little more complicated—some aren't naturally that way at all, not really kind, I mean—but they know Jesus came into the world to save it, to save it from sin, as we say—and they are very much aware of their sins—and they know that Jesus wants them to be kind to others, so they try to be. These people, like the rest of us, often mess up one way or another, but like the rest of us, they try. What with the hard lives some of them have had, it's a real struggle for them to be generous and pleasant instead of mean. They do so well, in fact, that I often wish the rest of the world could be at least like them; I think there would be fewer wars and less crime, and we would all be happier.

So it isn't fake?

> I guess it's bound to be, some of the time. But, no, it's usually a
> real sort of kind feeling toward the world in general. They're
> kind because God is kind to them. If you want to put it this way,
> they know their sins are forgiven.
>
> One time a man invited Jesus to eat with him. And while the
> group of men were eating, a woman from the streets came and
> wept at Jesus' feet. In fact, she was so overcome with his good-
> ness and her own sinfulness that she poured out perfume on
> his feet and wiped them with her hair. It's a powerful scene that
> this gospel describes. Jesus and that woman at his feet—moving.
>
> But the man who gave the dinner party was appalled and of-
> fended. "Do you know what kind of a woman this is?" he asked
> Jesus. But Jesus told him a story of two men who had borrowed
> money and couldn't repay it. The one who loaned them the
> money forgave the debts—one for fifty dollars, another for five
> hundred. Then he asked Simon, "Which of the two will love the
> banker more?"
>
> Simon, of course, said the one who had had five hundred dol-
> lars forgiven. Jesus said, "Right."
>
> What do you make of that?

I think that woman had met Jesus before—probably on the street—
and she realized he cared about her. Most other people told her to
get out of their face and away from their neighborhood, the way
Simon felt, even if he didn't say it. That's why she loved Jesus
and washed his feet. She loved him more than that man who gave
Jesus the dinner, I think.

> I think you're right. In fact, Jesus said to Simon that although
> the woman's sins were very many, they were all forgiven. Simon
> and his friends were amazed. But Jesus said that a person who
> had been forgiven a lot, would love a lot, and that people who
> were forgiven little couldn't love as much.

Oh, that gave that woman a lot of hope, I think. Did Jesus say any
more to her?

> No, he didn't even tell her to stop sinning. He just told her as
> he had said to Simon, that her sins were forgiven and she was
> saved.

I think she changed her life, whether it says so in the Bible or not. She might have changed to be like Mrs. Swanson, loving people so much—with kindness, I mean, not just sex.

I wish I could be like that. How do those last people you mentioned—the people here—know Jesus died for them?

> They hear the lessons from the Bible that tell us that. They sing the songs that tell us that. They learn to pray, and they experience that. Some have been converted at rallies of the church—revivals. But most of these people you see have never even been to a real revival. Faith comes to them in less dramatic ways.

Wow. That's cool. Maybe I should go to a revival sometime. Or maybe I should visit this church more. I think maybe some churches have a better spirit than others.

> It is terribly tempting to think that. But Jesus told us not to give in to that kind of thinking. He told a story once about a tax collector and a Pharisee.

A Pharisee? What's that?

> Most Pharisees were fine people in Jesus' time, like lots of the people in church today. But this Pharisee also thought he was better than others because he was smart in religion and because he really tried to obey all the rules in detail.

So, what did he do?

> Jesus said that this Pharisee was in the temple praying. And so was a tax-collector—which meant the kind of person most despised by the ordinary people, because they felt the Jewish tax collectors were traitors to the Jews, serving the Romans, the enemy, the way they did.

> Well, the Pharisee prayed—"O God, I thank you that I am not like other people." And the tax collector said in his prayer, "O God, be merciful to me, a sinner."

> And then Jesus said, "This tax collector went to his home justified." That means set right with God. And we can believe he was happy.

Oh, I wish I'd heard that story a long time ago. I think the Pharisee was probably a snob. Like the fake people that are in some churches.

What does the story mean to you? You said you wished you
had heard it before now.

I guess when I cry at night I'm also praying, "Be merciful to me
dear God. I'm a sinner." One time I was drunk and driving a
friend's car that I had borrowed, and I almost killed a little boy.
As it was, I smashed his bicycle. I was scared, but no one ever
knew it was me. But I knew. And God knew. I almost killed him.

I cried a lot for weeks after that. Just remembering that makes me
want to cry all over again. I was scared of everybody, because
everybody hated me, and I was afraid they'd catch me. I lived
from one day to the next feeling that way. Why can't I stop messing up?

One way or another we all mess up from time to time, even in
ways we don't realize. Knowing Jesus' stories and his love helps.

I'd like to say a prayer before you go.

Dear God, we are weak and lost much of the time. We are
sorrowful children instead of the strong and kind people you
want us to be. Thank you for what Jesus tried to teach us. Thank
you for what he did for us in his sacrifice on the cross. Thank
you for Jennie, and for friends, and for everything good and
beautiful. Thank you for the people of this church. And bless
with your cleansing and strengthening spirit this your servant
Elsena. In Jesus' name. Amen.

I hope you have a good evening and a good day tomorrow.

Thanks. And thanks for the stories. Bye.

Discussion Questions for Chapter 7

1. What are the ministries the church is providing to Elsena? Which ones
   are the most important?
2. In what ways could we say God is reaching out to Elsena? What are
   God's hopes for Elsena?
3. What people may turn out to have been important in Elsena's life if she
   finally makes it beyond her drinking?
4. If she fails, how would you evaluate her relationship to the congregation
   and the congregation's relationship to her?

5. Why is Elsena troubled about people being "fake"?
6. How do the story about Simon and the parable Jesus told about the Pharisee relate to your congregation and your faith?

8

What about Jesus?
A Visit with Newt

Newt comes in to his next meeting saying, "I think it is time we talked about Jesus." Baker agrees, and the two move rapidly ahead.

(Baker) What makes this so urgent?

(Newt) For one thing, you keep quoting him. For another, the New Testament focuses on him almost as much as on God.

Doesn't Jesus help you believe in God?

I'm not sure. I have a lot of questions about Jesus. He was, so far as I can tell, a remarkable man. He left an indelible mark on Western civilization. Whether he intended to or not, he started a movement that has lasted these last two millennia and keeps on growing. His religious teachings seem to have been powerfully communicated, especially in the earlier days when the crowds followed him. Later, they fell away. Instead of avoiding it as he could have, he seems to have faced his cruel death with great conviction and courage.

But what is all this extra baggage? You make Jesus out as something far more than an exceptionally charismatic leader and religious innovator. There seems to be no actual contemporary writing about Jesus. Paul's letters are the earliest material, and

Writing of Paul /Gospels

they ignore the man almost entirely. They proceed to build a theology around a transcendent Christ figure. The gospels, with a
biographical format, come later yet and are written as propaganda
more than as accurate reporting.

> You've really pursued this question. I'm impressed.

This Christ is associated with Jesus in ways I don't understand.
For example, you people say Jesus is "divine," as if he were somehow a part of God. And there's all this about his being one person
of a holy trinity of persons? Isn't that deifying a mortal, the way
the Romans did with their Caesars? Or the way—as I imagine
it—some of the Greek gods got a legendary start—from human
events lost in the mists of ancient history?

> You've done good homework. And your questions are all fair.
> Actually, you're more orthodox than you may realize. You root
> your questions in the real world, which is where faith belongs.
> Maintaining the humanity of this itinerant from Nazareth has
> been a profound concern for Christians since the earliest days.

Where else could they begin?

> Theologians wanted to make sure the Jesus story didn't spawn
> a mystery cult. Some believers made of Jesus an otherworldly
> god playacting the human life. That way, he never really lived
> and suffered and died. As you say, like the gods from Olympus.
> So their opponents, who won out, insisted on Jesus' humanity.
> In scripture, his lineage was specified, his hometown, and all
> the rest. In Gethsemane, he sweats blood. On the cross he thirsts.
> He cries out, "My God, why have you abandoned me?" Jesus
> was a very human being.

No problem in that. But what then is all the other stuff?

> We can get to that in a minute. But I want to emphasize an-
> other point. This is no mere antiquarian concern. A few modern-
> day Christians have said that it doesn't matter whether Jesus
> really lived or not. For them it's enough that the story forces us
> to examine our life and decide how we want to live, in good
> faith or bad faith.

I suppose their point is that you Christians believe a lot more than
one might necessarily infer from Jesus' historical life.

But to forget Jesus the man is to make a big mistake. It loses the anchor and allows the theological ship to drift along with almost any wind that blows.

At any rate, happily, you are starting with Jesus. In Jesus—and that means scripture is our main source—we have a tangible way to test dreamed up theology. Our faith has moral content and historical reality. If Jesus becomes only a heavenly figure drawing us away from the world instead of into its throbbing vitality, we can wander too far afield, far from the central Christian way of love and service. Any demagogue—with bland psychological reassurances or secret gnostic rituals—can play a tune and find dancers to follow. Debatable as we find the reported teachings and events of the story, Jesus still serves to keep our feet on the ground.

Now, back to the "stuff" as you call it. Are you really telling me you have no problem with Jesus so long as you don't have to take any church doctrine along with it?

Right. For the most part, I enjoy reading the gospel stories and Jesus' teachings. I don't mean I understand all the allusions to what went before him. I haven't studied up on Israel's history. And when the stories include miracles, as so many do, or that peculiar talk about the "last days" and the end of the world, I do get lost.

The miracles still? The rationalist in you keeps crowding out the poet, doesn't it? If it's any help, since the earliest times plenty of good Christians have not taken the miracles literally. Christians considered miracles more important as signs of meaning than mere wonderworks. They're for reflection, like other religious stories.

Some of the stories about healing seem real enough, like psychosomatic events of our own time. There's mystery in medicine even yet.

But religious language, even about healing, usually has a deeper purpose than a news reporter's account does. The stories inspire awe rather than the "wow" feeling you experience at a magic show: "Wow, how did he do that?"

I didn't mean to sidetrack us by mentioning miracles, but you're helpful.

Back to my larger concern: You keep Jesus human. But I don't think Christians say only that Jesus is a great teacher, leader, and a martyr. Like Socrates, maybe, or Lincoln. Aren't you watering down Christian belief terribly? I can't be content with just that and call myself Christian.

Oh, I'm not through.

There are a lot of ways of saying who is Christian. For an inclusive definition, we might say this: Christians are those who follow Jesus. If you could say just that much for yourself, that you follow Jesus, you've already made Jesus more than Socrates and Lincoln. You've made a life choice. It's impossible to follow two masters—at least when their paths diverge.

In the gospels, Jesus says, "Come, follow me." Following Jesus gives us a starting point from which we decide a lot of other things, such as whether Socrates or Lincoln were good, bad, or indifferent. And it puts us alongside other followers of Jesus, into a movement.

I wonder if that's my problem. I resist subservience. I won't agree to accept or obey doctrine on someone else's say so, to turn over my mind to someone else.

I hadn't thought of Jesus as heading a movement. Joining a movement is different from deciding which theological dogmas I want to accept.

I don't like to choose. A few of my Christian friends do make an either/or of belief in Jesus. They say I'm either for Jesus or against him. No one puts it that way about Abe Lincoln or Socrates. Usually, however, those friends—although they mean well—get under my skin.

They are too pushy?

They seem to think I'm lost until I can think of Jesus as being here and now, or in the next room. But what you say about a need for a starting point strikes me as true. When someone asks, "Why A," and I say, "Because B," and then they ask, "Why B," and I say, "Because C," and it goes on, "Why C" and "Why D" again and again farther and farther back, I eventually come to a place I have to say "Just because." I find a starting point. I could see Jesus embodying that for me, better than Lincoln or Socrates.

What about Jesus? A Visit with Newt

Who was Jesus, to your mind?

> That's an old question, isn't it? But it's new for each when we ask it.
>
> The disciples had to wrestle with it. In one of the gospel stories Jesus asks them point blank, "Who do you think I am?"
>
> As you say, especially in the last two hundred years, hundreds of scholars have tried to describe the historical Jesus. But always people have tried to answer the identity question the way you pose it. "Who was Jesus?" That's why we have four gospels—each writer wanted to put it his way. So we have a lot of variations on the answer.
>
> Incidentally, I have to be away for a week. Before I leave, I think I'll collect some of the answers for you—ancient and modern—and put them in the mail. The range is fascinating. Even at your present place in doubt and faith, you might accept some of them.

What do you think I could accept? All I've said is that Jesus was remarkably powerful as a religious figure and something, I dare say, of a rebel.

> I'm still thinking of the starting point interpretation of Jesus. And I'm thinking of your apparent agreement when we talked about the two kinds of truth. As children, I think, we allow for the poetic and the mysterious better than we do after the age of reason. "unless you (trust, believe ...) like a child you will not enter the kingdom of God ..."

In that sense we've reentered an adolescent period since the Enlightenment.

> Yes. Nowadays we want everything spelled out and simple and single in meaning, the way it is in elementary Newtonian physics.
>
> On the way to the richer depths of human understanding, I guess many of us have to go through a Newtonian period. The world becomes a mechanical machine, complex enough to be fascinating. But so much is squeezed out of the world if it is only that. At least granting the reality of Jesus' influence is a step beyond that. There's a lot more, of course. But if I start my moral commitment and my understanding of true virtue with

Jesus, I can't go far wrong. And I would call that a step of Christian faith that you've taken already.

You're more than a bystander, Newt. There's passion in your search. "I would be true, for there are those who trust me, I would be pure, for there are those who care"; do you know that hymn?

Yes, as a matter of fact, I do. It's full of naive and noble sentiments and is utterly unsingable.

I'm trying to be patient, but you will get to my basic question, I hope—about the divinity of Christ? Is Jesus a god or a man?

To me, Jesus Christ is the fulcrum of meaning. In that sense he is messiah ("Christ" in Greek), which means anointed, to deliver us from otherwise agnostic confusion. He is the norm by which I make judgments, the north on my compass.

All that means an enormous turning about for my life. Instead of getting ahead, I am asked to empty myself, become a servant. I am asked to honor the poor and the poor in spirit, the meek, those who mourn. I am asked to turn the other cheek, not to be anxious, not to judge. I am asked to accept crucifixion as a possibility for my life rather than life, liberty, and the mere pursuit of fame, fortune, and happiness. I am even asked to forgive and affirm my enemy. The Christian is asked to follow Jesus—and die to the self in so doing.

I hesitate to say any of that, because I can make no claim to realize it in my moral and spiritual self. I do often try. And I pray for help to try more often, to make it my inner selfhood, in fact.

Are you claiming to answer my question?

It may be. You see, these admonitions all run counter to my natural instincts for self-preservation and self-aggrandizement. That being the case—that I assign authority and reality to these sentiments—I find I can and want to sing the hymns to Jesus and say the old creeds in their various christological languages quite happily. They come from different epochs. Sometimes Jesus is Messiah. Sometimes he is "of one substance with the Father," which is what you designate as "divine," I presume. Sometimes he is an elder brother who suffered terribly and knows the trouble I've seen. These testimonies to the Christ of faith—as people often put it—are expressions of what I see as fundamental in the universe, tied in with truth and reality as firmly as anything you could point to in the physics laboratory.

But was Jesus divine? Was his essence different from that of any other creature?

We've already said he was a mortal. The metaphysics of divine substance was evidently meaningful to people of ages past. I don't believe it is for the person on the street today. It isn't for me. That may be our loss, but I doubt it's reversible. But I can't change the century I live in. As I say, however, I understand it enough to sing it in poetic hymnody and speak it in liturgical prose. I am often deeply moved as I do. I can use "divinity"—meaningfully—in in-house theological talk. But for pedestrian discussion, I use it sparingly. If it means to assert that Jesus has a unique role in my life, unlike that of any other persons, I most definitely say yes. YES! However, if you're organizing to anathematize people who won't call Jesus of Nazareth divine, all the while trying to follow him, count me out.

I think I understand. But unless I have missed something, you haven't said anything about being saved by Jesus. That's a big part of the language too. Christians talk about redemption and atonement and getting right with God. I hear talk like that a lot in some churches I visit.

Touché. You'll be a better theologian than I'll ever be, once you believe.

In that question you raise all kinds of issues—about the nature of human beings and about the human condition. Do we need to be saved, whatever that means? Are you and I corrupted or stuck in so serious a situation that we can't get out by ourselves, so serious that we need rescuing? I answer yes. And it's my experience that God—the God I know through Jesus—rescues me. I believe that. I grant, however, that this may make no sense whatever to you. You may not have any experience like that.

On the contrary, those times when I'm lost and feel almost damned—that's pretty close to how I feel. I thought atonement was for sins committed or duties neglected, and someone had to pay.

> No, that's much too narrow. Sin is better used in the singular, a condition. It's a cloud over the world preventing sunlight, a wrongness within the human soul. It is a state of being—from which we are rescued. I could sum up the gospel this way perhaps: "I believe in sin's pervasive reality. And that reality is overcome by God's power, something that for me is seen and wrought in Jesus Christ." And I believe we're forgiven. That's the sequence we celebrate every week at one point in the liturgy—confession and the assurance of pardon.

It does all fit together, doesn't it, once you've stepped over into this language—this assumption of God?

> Yes, it often does, in moving ways. But there are other metaphors for the sin-salvation experience. One place the New Testament will have darkness overturned by light; another oppression replaced by liberation; and in yet another, death defeated by resurrection. I recently read a book called *The Golgotha Earthquake* by Paul Minear. It uses three different New Testament books, Hebrews, Matthew, and a Pauline letter. They're almost three different languages. But they all hinge on Christ and what he did for the Christian.

But where does all that understanding come from? You can't derive sin and a need for salvation from the hard sciences, that's for sure. Our social sciences want us to stop talking sin and be free of guilt; to them guilt is a sickness, eroding mental health.

> Where does this understanding come from? Do we need the word revelation again—a message from outside ourselves? We can't count on sin to seek its own reform. It's too self-deceiving. In Christ, however, people have seen undiluted virtue and, at the same time, their own sin. Christ the judge is the Savior because he shows the world its guilt.

> I'm well into the area of inside formulations of the faith, so I'm probably not helpful.

I need to get on home, I'm sorry to say. Let me mull over what you've said. You've been talking as if I were an insider, and I don't mind. This isn't all public theology; you would have lost my worldly friends early on. But I think I've followed you not only in my head, but somehow with my heart as well. Have a good trip.

Discussion Questions for Chapter 8

1. Is Baker's approach satisfactory to you as you think about helping people like Newt find their way into faith? Would you prefer more emphasis on the divinity of Christ, even for the novice who resists it?

2. How important would the miracle stories be if you were to write a gospel account of Jesus?

3. Baker mentions Christians who say that there could be Christianity if we had only the story of Jesus, had he not really lived. How does that strike you?

4. Baker attempts a definition of who is a Christian. What would your definition be?

5. Discuss the answers that can be given to Newt while he still thinks of himself as outside the church. Some answers are only understandable on the assumption that God is a reality. For example, the history of Jesus' time and the story of his life can be recounted for both the believer and the skeptic, but the story of Christ's death for sinners on the cross is more of an in-house matter, if it is to be understood.

6. What are the various reasons Newt might be resisting faith in Jesus as Christ besides the improbability of the incarnation?

9

A Letter to Newt

Dear Newt,

Here are the selections I promised.

The first of these may or may not be by Saint Paul himself. It was probably written not earlier than thirty years after the crucifixion. (The scholars who question the authorship cite internal literary style; ascribing literature to well-known persons was commonplace in the first century. You can see that it did not take long for the community to understand Jesus in a very exalted terms.)

"Firstborn of all creation" must come from a person who finds truly cosmic change wrought by Christ.

In Christ, says the writer, God

has rescued us from the power of darkness and transferred us into the kingdom of his beloved Son, in whom we have redemption, the forgiveness of sins. He is the image of the invisible God, the firstborn of all creation; for in him all things in heaven and on earth were created, things visible and invisible, whether thrones or dominions or rulers or powers–all things have been created through him and for him. He himself is before all things, and in him all things hold together. He is the head of the body, the church; he is the beginning, the firstborn from the dead, so that he might come to have first place in everything. For in him all the fullness of God was pleased to dwell, and through him

God was pleased to reconcile to himself all things, whether on earth or in heaven, by making peace through the blood of his cross. (Colossians 1:13–20 NRSV)

According to tradition, the next excerpt is from a Galilean fisherman, the apostle John, although the scholars doubt it for many reasons. These "Johannine" writings—the gospel, the book of Revelation, and the three short letters of John just before it—appear interconnected in their content and style. The researchers attribute them to a "school" from Asia Minor, at least distantly related to the witness of John, one of the Twelve.

You already know these first paragraphs of John—that poetic section (the prologue, we call it) about the logos or word. You heard it Christmas Eve when you visited our congregation. In the climax to that section comes the classic assertion of the incarnation: "And the word became flesh and dwelt among us."

The true light, which enlightens everyone, was coming into the world. He was in the world, and the world came into being through him; yet the world did not know him. He came to what was his own, and his own people did not accept him. But to all who received him, who believed in his name, he gave power to become children of God, who were born, not of blood or of the will of the flesh or the will of man, but of God. And the Word became flesh and lived among us, and we have seen his glory, the glory as of a father's only son, full of grace and truth. (John 1:9–14 NRSV)

This can be supplemented with early words in the first Johannine epistle. Talk about poetic language as against the prosaic!

We declare to you what was from the beginning, what we have heard, what we have seen with our eyes, what we have looked at and touched with our hands, concerning the word of life—this life was revealed, and we have seen it and testify to it, and declare to you the eternal life that was with the Father and was revealed to us—we declare to you what we have seen and heard so that you also may have fellowship with us; and truly our fellowship is with the Father and with his Son Jesus Christ. We are writing these things so that our joy may be complete. (1 John 1:1–4 NRSV)

As in the gospel's prologue, here again Christ is portrayed as part of God's action in the world from the beginning of time.

Earlier, Saint Paul had told a similar story in moving words, stressing moral content as well as metaphysical self-humbling by Christ. This is from his letter to the Philippians.

> Let the same mind be in you that was in Christ Jesus, who, though he was in the form of God, did not regard equality with God as something to be exploited, but emptied himself, taking the form of a slave being born in human likeness. And being found in human form, he humbled himself and became obedient to the point of death even death on a cross. Therefore God also highly exalted him and gave him the name that is above every name, so that at the name of Jesus every knee should bend, in heaven and on earth and under the earth, and every tongue should confess that Jesus Christ is Lord, to the glory of God the Father. (Philippians 2:5–11 NRSV)

I want to add now excerpts that reflect a little of the modern world's attempts to interpret Jesus. The French scholar Ernst Renan attempted a life of Jesus in 1861. He was accused, as you might expect, of being an "unbeliever." He ends his book with the section below. See what you think. He follows Jesus, but he rejects the language of the orthodox tradition.

> This sublime person, who each day still presides over the destiny of the world, we may call divine, not in the sense that Jesus has absorbed all the divine, or has been adequate to it, (to employ an expression of the schoolmen) but in the sense that Jesus is the one who has caused his fellow-men to make the greatest step towards the divine…In him was condensed all that is good and elevated in our nature. He was not sinless; he has conquered the same passions that we combat; no angel of God comforted him, except his good conscience; no Satan tempted him, except that which each one bears in his heart. In the same way that many of his great qualities are lost to us, through the fault of his disciples, it is also probable that many of his faults have been concealed. But never has any one so much as he made the interest of humanity predominate in his life over the littleness of self-love…Jesus only lived for his

Father and the divine mission which he believed he was
destined to serve...Whatever may be the unexpected phe-
nomena of the future, Jesus will not be surpassed. (*The
Life of Jesus*, London: Ballantyne Press, 1863, 310f.)

Another perspective is from a Connecticut Yankee, Horace
Bushnell, from the same historical period. Bushnell, both
preacher/theologian and civic leader, was a gifted interpreter of
Christian dogma to those who, like himself, rejected an old and
brittle Calvinism. This exerpt summarizes his "moral theory" of
Christ's work.

(Jesus) works by no fiat of absolute will as when God said
"let there be light." He respects your moral nature, doing
it no violence. He moves on your consent, by moving on
your convictions, wants, sensibilities, and sympathies. He
is the love of God, the beauty of God, the mercy of God—
God's whole character, brought nigh through a proper and
true Son of Man, a nature fellow to your own, thus to reno-
vate and raise your own. Meeting you at your fall and
disorder, as being himself incarnated into the corporate
evil of your state, he brings you God's great feeling to work
on yours...And that he may get the greater and more con-
straining power over you, he reveals to you by his suffering death, the suffering state of God's perfection—stung
by the wrongs, and moved in holy grief for the sad and
shameful lot of his fallen children. His suffering was in
fact the tragic hour of divine goodness; for what to our
slow feeling is even eternal goodness till we see it tragically moved? Nay, it was even necessary, if transgressors
were to have their dull heart opened to this goodness, that
they should see it persecuted and gibbeted by themselves.
Thus, and therefore, he dies, raising by his death at our
hands those terrible convictions that will rend our bosom
open to his love—dies for love's sake in love for us. (New
York: Charles Scribner, 1864, *Christ and Salvation*, 88f.)

Better known as a German musician and a missionary physician in Africa, Albert Schweitzer was also a pioneering New Testament scholar. At the end of his long and highly significant study,
first published in 1906, and later in English as *The Quest of the
Historical Jesus*, Schweitzer concluded that Jesus focused his

message on the apocalyptic coming of the kingdom and therefore is almost inaccessible to us who cannot operate on the same assumptions. Yet Jesus comes to us and wins us for disciples. The final two paragraphs are widely quoted.

> Jesus as a concrete historical personality remains a stranger to our time, but His spirit, which lies hidden in His words, is known in simplicity, and its influence is direct...He was not teacher, not a casuist; He was an imperious ruler. It was because He was so in his inmost being that He could think of Himself as the Son of Man. That was only the temporally conditioned expression of the fact that He was an authoritative ruler. The names in which men expressed recognition of Him as such, Messiah, Son of Man, Son of God, have become for us historical parables. We can find no designation which expresses what he is for us.

> He comes to us as One unknown, without a name, as of old, by the lake-side, He came to those men who knew Him not. He speaks to us the same word: "Follow thou me!" and he sets us to tasks which He has to fulfill for our time. He commands. And to those who obey Him, whether they be wise or simple, He will reveal Himself in the toils, the conflicts, the sufferings which they shall pass through in His fellowship, and, as an ineffable mystery, they shall learn in their own experience Who He is. (New York: The MacMillan Company, 1948, trans. W. Montgomery, 402f.)

Martin Dibelius, a leading German scholar, doing a critical study of Jesus in the late 1930s, accepted critical New Testament study fully but held out a crucial role for Jesus as God's sign in sections such as the following:

> Doubt, or unbelief, does not consist of a skeptical attitude toward one or more things related in the New Testament; for even if the events did not take place just as they are described there, what did take place can nevertheless be God's sign, and so can the account of it, fragmentary as it may be or burdened with contemporary views and ideas. Unfaith really consists in a refusal to recognize the event— and the account of it—as a true sign of God's actuality, and then to dedicate one's life to it. Along with this attitude one may of course look upon the Gospels as good,

interesting, beautiful and worthwhile books; indeed one may confer upon them and upon the Man of whom they tell, the highest human titles of honor. But none of these high evaluations and appreciations can even touch the decisive question of whether or not God gave a sign. (*Jesus*, Philadelphia: Westminster, 1949, trans. Charles B. Hedrick and Frederick C. Grant, 135.)

I will add a few other sentences as a footnote on the relation of history to the transhistorical portrayals of Jesus (the annointed one, the Messiah, the Christ). In an essay of 1959, Hans Conzelman wrote about the historical Jesus and that interpretive dimension we have inadequately called the poetic. You may skip over this as the insider's God-talk that it is if it seems meaningless to you.

In its own understanding, the church takes for granted that the Risen One is the Crucified One; the Risen One is firmly held to be none other than Jesus of Nazareth. This is true for both basic types of New Testament Christology. It is true in the Hellenistic-Pauline Christology where the historical material from the life of Jesus is ignored—up to the (single point) of his having existed. It also is true in the Synoptic Gospels where faith is illustrated through a collection of remembered material. Thus, according to the church's understanding, Jesus remains the presupposition of faith. This, then, prevents mythologizing the figure of the Redeemer.

The lines cross at the point of the resurrection. This is regarded by the church as an event in space and time…(H)istory cannot establish the facticity of the Resurrection. It can only establish that men testified that they had seen Jesus alive after his death. In this experience they find the key to the meaning of his death…Theology can postulate no historical facts. (*Jesus*, Philadelphia: Fortress Press, 1973, trans. J. Raymond Lord, 93 f.)

The agenda of our meetings keeps extending itself. We may need more conversations than I realized. But I enjoy them, so let's persevere. But keep guiding the agenda yourself, as you have been doing.

Best wishes,
Baker

Discussion Questions for Chapter 9

1. Which of these quotations comes nearest to what you would like to set down if you were a writer or teacher?

2. Which would you think might be of help to Newt from what you know of him?

3. What would the "emptying" of yourself, if you were to follow the admonition in Philippians 2, mean in your attitudes and your life? How would you interpret Christ to a congregation in a sermon using this passage?

4. Plan a dialogue or role play around the theme of how God caught the people off-guard with a crucified Messiah.

5. In this material that Baker sent to Newt, what are the various questions you can imagine that lie behind the excerpts, coming from their different epochs and contexts?

10

Jesus Christ:
A Visit with Newt

Baker, back from a trip, finds Newt eager to continue.

(Newt) The Jesus readings came, as you promised. Thanks. You were right; "diverse" they were.

> (Baker) It's not easy to put them all in the same basket, to find a real unity in them.

Right. All told, the more grandiose contend that a cosmic sea change came with Jesus. The whole of history, the world's relation to the fundamental reality of God is changed. The more modest say that the change came in the followers and the believers.

Three other things I notice: People seem to relate personally to Jesus as if he were alive, not just a historical figure. Secondly, at least in what you sent, there's little of the metaphysics talk that befuddles me.

In fact—and this is the third thing—I discovered with some more reading on my own that there's an enormous variety of metaphors for Christ. There isn't just one term that's exclusively accepted. It's as if the New Testament writers couldn't find enough images to say what they thought of Jesus. He's the Word of God, they say. I take it that might mean message, not in what he says, but in himself. Or he's a priest, a special high priest. He's a ransom, or a sacrificial lamb who "died for our sins," as people say. He's the source of salvation.

In the other things I've read, people tried to say what Christ had done, more than who he was metaphysically. I want to know why we can't say he was a mortal, within history, in whom people can find a starting standpoint for looking at the rest of history and all its questions. God, if God there be, gave us in Christ a fulcrum with which we can bend history—for better or worse. We have that freedom.

> Very interesting. I like your imagination. One comment: Putting it as you do sounds a little as if Jesus appeared in a historical vacuum. To me, Christ's advent was more solid. People didn't first see Jesus and then ask themselves what metaphors they could find that might apply to him. They already lived in a culture that interpreted reality in terms of creation and redemption, sacrifice and atonement, the covenant and godly promises of a coming deliverer. Time was moving forward toward freedom, justice, and peace. Then, encountering Jesus, they declared, "Ah, yes. Here he is."

> Then later, as you say, other metaphors were taken up for the interpretive task, particularly from philosophy.

Tell me, do you think a person could get at all this Christ business without that three-person-one-God conundrum? That trinitarian malarkey?

> And still follow Jesus, which was my minimal definition for Christians? Probably so, if you can tolerate Christians who will keep using the "malarkey" as you call it. That formula dates right back into the New Testament, although most of the "metaphysics talk" comes later. The trinitarian formula not only links us to the past, it also defines God for us. It says, God is of this kind, not of that kind. God is of the kind who creates the earth and the human race and the universe and calls it all "good," not bad. The same God provides the unique self-disclosure and promised sustenance that we know in Jesus and the Spirit. "Triune" defines for us a relational God who reaches out in redemptive love and care.

What do you think a nonmetaphysical christology or Christ dogma would be?

If I came to believe it, that is? Well, it would still have to indicate the essential change that came with Jesus. Christians certainly assert more than that Jesus was an unusual person. They want to say more than that he founded a new religion. They mean that for them he brought a change in the way things most basically are. Jesus' cross accomplished something very basic. I don't see it myself. Nonetheless, that's the gist of half the literature you sent me.

One of my questions is this: It looks like all this means that God— or reality itself—changes. Would you say this too—that God changes, with the shift from B.C. to A.D.? Or C.E., they say now.

Hold on. You're too far ahead of me. By a nonmetaphysical christology, I judge, we mean one in which Jesus still plays a crucial role for the believer?

Yes.

That would be the case, for example, if we said Jesus was a unique moral example whose fidelity and selflessness transform us?

Hmmm. Truly unique? A moral hero who defines moral virtues for all times and places? That could be a rich and strong portrait, but I'm not sure. Maybe it's too intellectual. It seems pallid; it lacks something.

Yes. Even though there's a lot of truth in that moral hero talk. But, as you say, it doesn't capture our Christian experience fully. It doesn't match the liturgical tradition, either.

If you had to do it, how would you express the idea of Christ without trinity-talk?

I think I've already mentioned an option that I find helpful, and you've almost said as much too. The approach speaks of the whole phenomenon of Jesus as a crucial historical event, crucial for our sense of all other history. This "Christ-event" centers in Jesus, but it's broader than Jesus' brief ministry. It includes the long preparation time of Israel's history before Jesus. It includes the resurrection experiences of the disciples and the rise of the church way beyond Israel.

Holding this view, I can say God revealed divine judgment and mercy in the man Jesus and that his followers find this to be true right down to the present. And that's my real experience, actually.

And, I'm beginning to think, mine too, much as I resist it.

And, unlike that moral hero theory, it does more justice to the sea-change you mention. It feels more continuous with the traditions of worship and church doctrine. It assumes we humans are historical beings given, by an encounter in time, a saving guidance for our own lifework and destiny. This is more than intellectual learning. Taking our fundamental life-clue from Jesus this way does change us. Following Jesus becomes a health-giving, saving insight, a transforming loyalty. Does that side-step your troubled metaphysical questions about the Trinity?

You say "Christ-event" includes Israel's history. Surely you're not reading Jesus into the Hebrew Bible the way some preachers do. They say prophets had an inside track on knowledge of what Jesus would end up being and doing.

No. Not that way. But as I said, Israel evolved a culture that made possible the Jesus we know. The long evolution of Jewish sacrifice tradition, for example, contributes to the Jesus story. Implicitly, Abraham and Isaac are there in the Jesus story. Moses and the exodus and Passover are part of it. So, too, Isaiah with his poetry of the suffering servant. This culture of Israel undergirds the rise of Christianity, especially its understanding of suffering and the cross.

Does this divine self-disclosure, as you call it, rule out other views of God? Not everyone finds Christ-talk helpful. It's not understood even among some of my friends—some folks I call generic religionists. They're decent people and spiritually motivated, but they wouldn't call themselves Christian believers. They think it narrows their options. Can you help them?

I can understand that. They react against a fundamentalist mindset, as do I. The fundamentalist mindset wants to rule out conflicting belief and thereby bolster its own security. It would say yes to your question about ruling out other views of God. "No other name than that of Jesus can save us." You can see in that, of course, both profound conviction of Jesus' importance and an element of defensiveness.

I believe a more secure faith opens itself to others who are serious seekers and does not damn them. It concentrates on finding the truths of God. Start with the Jews—we live alongside them in Christianity, both of us to heirs God's promises and grace. In that reactionary exclusivist view, people forget that Jesus was a Jew.

Now, I think you had a different question when I interrupted you.

Yes. I was trying to say a strong christology believes the world to be basically changed in Jesus; but then, thinking of God and the vastness of the created universe, I couldn't imagine God changing. Does God change?

Philosophically, of course, the answer is almost bound to be no. God is the very principle of constancy. On the other hand, if we use "God" to mean the totality of all that is, God is constantly evolving.

I once saw a bushel of snails in a Marseilles market—from a distance. It seemed to be a mass of constant movement—like something out of a science fiction movie. I'll bet the seething universe is like that—constant in its entirety, but internally all evolving motion.

That paradox may be the best we can do.

God has to be more than abstract principle. Throughout scripture, God is personal. That means two-way conversation. God does react. In the Bible stories, God not only hardens Pharaoh's heart. God's own heart hardens. God repents. God loves and does not grow weary. Such human images and stories point to a living God. People have even dared to say God suffers.

In cyber-lingo, we would say God is interactive, not "read only."

So God changes? I have heard it said that before Jesus divine wrath predominates. After Jesus, the anger is gone. All is forgiven.

That's much too simple. God is not only within time, for one thing, but beyond it, too, if that makes any sense to you. For another, long before Jesus' time, God was known to be merciful and long-suffering. Read Hosea. "How can I give you up, O Ephraim?" Read the psalms. God "forgives all our iniquities."

We do use language about God's mercy as if Christ's death changes God. In prayer, too, we use language that appears to ask for change in God. If the personal quality of the God-relation is to be expressed verbally, and if we are to be honest in prayer, that language is virtually inevitable.

To our minds, God is high and transcendent. But God is not passive and remote. God comes near to us, especially in Jesus.

As a kid, I liked the rhythm of a Bible verse I didn't understand: "My thoughts are not your thoughts," said God, "nor my ways your ways."

Right. And that is nowhere better demonstrated than in Jesus. Jesus wasn't the messiah people expected—and wanted. He didn't destroy Roman rule; he restored no throne to Israel.

And this is the scandal of the cross. So unexpected. The crucified Messiah shows us a vulnerable God. Jesus points to—and he himself embodies—God's vulnerability. Jesus yields himself for others in infinite compassion. He preaches and lives out a corresponding ethic—the other cheek, the second mile. He teaches us to emulate God's patience—a patience that sends rain and sun for both the evil and good among us. Far more, this Jesus offers himself to die for the ungodly. That is a victimized, mangled Messiah we see being crucified, a vulnerable God.

No wonder it takes people awhile to believe. This is no mere philosopher's First Mover or clever moralist urging human virtue. This is not tame doctrine. This God is no mere clockmaker, setting the universe on its automatic track. You're saying this strange God comes and lives and suffers in our human lives, yielding and exposed.

Yes. And therefore, too, this is no God to be conjured up from an armchair conversation like this. The story is all so much more alive than that.

If I let myself go, I can move into that scene. We ourselves are vulnerable; that's why Jesus speaks to us so profoundly. That's what you're saying, isn't it? We can't claim to control our lives a hundred percent. We know AIDS and accidents, tumors and terrors of the mountains, and flooding of the rivers. But I never conceived God that way, the broken, bloodied Creator. I have to think about that a while.

> Yes. Sometimes I think Christianity is outlandish and insane. At other times, I call it amazingly daring. It's full of the unexpected. Jesus, the King, chooses the grimey poor to lunch with. Jesus turns everything upside down. He asks me to identify with the outcast, right alongside the high achiever, the idiot alongside the gifted, and the gutter drunk alongside the good-guy social pillar. I enjoy the privileged folk as companions; Jesus dismisses them: "They have their reward."

A bloodied Creator and Jesus the Son of God lunching with the poor. Whatever people get out of this story, it's not a program of success through self-esteem and gladhanding, is it?

> No. It's too realistic.

Realistic? I wasn't being facetious. How can this viewpoint be of use to us?

> That's not the point, is it?

But we need self-esteem. You don't really believe that this guilt system Christians promulgate is healthy, do you? New Age theologies may be weird, but at least they don't inflict us with guilt. Our need to be affirmed far outweighs our need to be forgiven, don't you think?

> No, I really do believe that a guilt system, as you call it, is a truer reading of the human situation than the human potential hope of self-affirmation. Of course there's a neurotic guilt, which is to be avoided and healed; but unless we're never going to probe beneath the surface, unless we avoid moral questions altogether, we will one day discover the need for our own repentance and for God's mercy. We're not billiard balls, each sufficient to itself, clicking innocently against each other. We're part and parcel of a body of humanity that has enslaved and murdered and swindled members of its own body since time began—and still does, day upon day upon day even now.

Surely there are healthy-minded people who don't need repentance and all that. My everyday world is full of them.

Is it? Behind all the smiling "have-a-nice-day" countenances you don't think there lurks grief and shame and discouragement and pain? Christianity provokes in most of us enough moral sensitivity that we all learn firsthand about sin.

I'll tell you a simple, simple story. A white man lives in an interracial neighborhood. He's proud to be so liberal and socially responsible. One morning he meets a black youth at the door, who wants to be paid much too well for a trivial job of shoveling away a light snow. He makes the bargain anyway, feeling cheated. Next day, after an ice storm, another African American comes to his door, this one an adult, desperately needing work, insisting he can chip away the ice that has accumulated on the walks. The homeowner says, "I doubt it," but they set a modest price for the work.

An hour later the worker reports in, admitting he could't manage the ice. He has done some other shoveling, however, which the householder didn't want done. The employer rejects the workman's plea for full pay and gives something less. The black man leaves, sad and embittered. Only later does the white man realize his own pettiness. He had not for a minute put himself in the shoes of the transient laborer. He had not for even a moment thought of the worker as one whom God loves, for whom Christ died. But he calls himself a Christian. And he recognizes another instance in the vast and compounded morass of interracial vindictiveness.

Is this an exaggerated, neurotic guilt complex or a sign of the human condition?

The man is a racist, that's all. I doubt he would have been the same toward white workers. Also, he let the encounter with the youth affect his response to the adult the way we all do, the way we kick the dog after a hard day at the office. Otherwise your story wouldn't have mentioned it. He was stingy with his money rather than generous. He lacked imagination and couldn't get outside himself. I think I could go on and on.

Notice, he can't be forgiven by the one he wronged. The black man has vanished back into anonymity. If the householder is morally serious, he can't dismiss the event. Experiences like this accumulate. He will end in despair that erodes his better intentions, or he will need to find forgiveness of some sort. Sin like that infests the landscape—from prudery and pettiness to grievous mendacity and greed and self-deception.

Oh, we can make a lot of proposals for that white man. None of them will last, however, unless he finds both forgiveness and the power to turn a corner. That has to happen over and over and over in a Christian life.

Don't be too hard on the man. I could see myself there.

I was there, of course. And I remembered those words from the old prayerbook. (Frankly I am sorry they took them out in our later versions—they probably thought the words were psycho-logically ill-advised.) "There is no health in us," the prayer said. I need God in my innermost soul, to forgive me and set me going again. I don't merely want God to give me a moral ex-ample in Jesus. I want to know God has won the battle and fundamentally changed the way things are. I want to know that God has set me right again, that I am accepted by the divine presence and governance of all that is.

That's my sermon for the day. Tell me what you're thinking.

The more I think about human intransigence, the more I see the need for a turn-around. God, if God is more than wishful think-ing, might be part of an answer. Compassion is necessary; it isn't simply a nice aspect of the God-image. We need an active recon-ciliation of the human reality with whatever is holy. If God cares, we could say Jesus makes that into truth we can feel in our bones.

You seem to make sin very broad. It isn't just moral trespass?

Not in my book. It's what oppresses us—fear of death, ungrate-ful rejection of our created human limits, our moral duplicity, the cynicism that makes life meaningless and empty.

The shrinks and therapists may be on to something broader themselves these days. Instead of just pointing to the guilts we accumulate, they say we need an affirmation that overcomes shame. Somewhere deep down we feel exposed, aware of our alienation from the original health of creation and from what we were intended to be. That's shame.

The word "shame" doesn't occur there, but read Job 38 some-time. After all his justified self-justifications, reminding God of

Job's true innocence in the face of so much suffering, Job says, in effect, I will shut my mouth. I have been presumptuous, even in my innocence. I am ashamed. He has seen the majesty of God.

Without an intuition of that grand backdrop of God's magnificence and creation's glories, we do just count little—or large—sins. We short-change our estimates of human life and its meaning, almost to the point of pettiness. There's a much larger meaning for reconciliation than racking up indulgences that erase a list of sins.

Wow. How we got into this, I'm not sure. We started talking about the change wrought by what you have named the Christ-event. Then we spoke of God's changelessness and God's vulnerability in a crucified Messiah. Then we talked of sin and we were back to God's transcendence.

With all this about Christ, I'm led back to one more question, although it will have to wait till next time, if you're willing. What about Buddha? That's back out in public theology I guess. We've been getting pretty deeply into insider-talk, wouldn't you say?

Yes, we have. But you've kept up with me. Sorry, I did talk too much.

Discussion Questions for Chapter 10

1. How important is the doctrine of the Trinity in your own religious tradition?
2. How would you respond to Newt's question, "Does God change?"
3. How important are the Hebrew scriptures (the Old Testament) in your Christian faith?
4. Would you argue that guilt feelings are a natural part of the human condition or something that healthy-minded people can avoid? How about feelings of "shame" as Baker uses the word?
5. In words that are your own, how would you describe the role or place of Jesus the Messiah, the Christ, in your life?

11

At Sea:
A Visit with April

Baker is on a plane flight, seated next to April, an energetic conversational-ist and, it turns out, something of a seeker.

(Baker) You say you're from Boulder. That's a scenic place to grow up.

(April) Lots of people say that. To me, of course, it's just a home-town.

I suppose that's so. I was there once. I liked the mountain views, and the pedestrian streets, good climate. It reminded me of Berkeley, somehow—Berkeley, California.

I grew up in Boulder, but I went East for school. Some of my class-mates went to Berkeley, though. I visited them. It's a freer spirit out there. Especially Southern California.

A freer spirit?

Oh, you know. They aren't so uptight about cultural norms. I think the climate helps. And beaches. We get closed in by the winter in Massachusetts, as well as by the prissy social norms.

Or, like, the problem of careerism.

Careerism?

Yeah. I have a cousin who's a doctor, and she wants to have a baby and then work part-time. She told me it's very hard to think of a doctor part-time. The work pattern all assumes full-timers. That's careerism. It can be a drag.

My boyfriend is only a junior, and he gets it worse than I do. They don't bug women as much. He says all his relatives and older friends are on his back about what he's going to do. They want him to commit himself to a career—like this idea of choosing a major at college. Clyde says that's not what life is about. I think Clyde's right.

And what is life about?

Well, I guess it's fulfilling yourself. That's the main way to enjoying life as I see it. That could include kids and even something of a career, if you really like what you're doing. It wouldn't include having a career for the sake of having a career, if you get what I mean.

I understand, thanks to my own children. I was afraid they wouldn't make a living, even.

People are hung up on making a living. That's why I like California—they just coast along.

You'd probably fit a lot better in California than I would. The Californian I know best seems confused to me, but maybe it's my problem, not his. He's so New Age I can't keep up—doesn't seem to walk on the ground. He's always changing from one pursuit to another—one job or hobby to another—photography, then landscape gardening, then finding a part in a movie somewhere. Adequate income while it lasts, but undependable.

Sounds pretty interesting to me. I get tired of one single thing after a while. Some Californians have made a lot by being available to try out something undependable. Look at this computer magazine. It has an article on Silicon Valley and Steve Jobs—the guy who founded Apple Computer. Lots of these computer guys were dropouts. They don't think about careers and degrees.

Careers and degrees can do a lot to stifle creativity, wouldn't you say?

I'd have to hear cases, I guess. The Yankees and New England history gave our history a lot of creative energy and channeled it pretty well, don't you think?

The Puritans also repressed a lot of their natural instincts, it seems to me. In my next life, I won't opt for that one, if I have my druthers.

You're already planning your next life, at your young age? You must have young friends who talk reincarnation.

Yes. I have. I'm not as serious as they are, though.

But you partly believe in it, you mean.

Oh, I think everybody does. Age doesn't have a lot to do with it. Like—I've never been to Ireland, but I'm almost convinced I lived there in a former life—probably about the tenth century.

Actually a larger proportion of the population than you'd think shares that belief with me. But I don't believe in astrology. My roommate does. She thinks the stars, thousands and even millions of light years away, have something to do with her destiny. She reads the horoscope nearly every day. It's not just a joke with her.

And she's going to an Ivy League school!

Yes. I can't understand her really. When I was in yoga, they had mystical talk that was pretty far out. Meridians, chi energy. You find stuff like that in massage and those barefoot medics in China. But at least it had a here and now result—better health. You could tell that. Like acupuncture. How do you explain that in our medical terms? It's almost like astrology, I sometimes think. Then other times, I go for it totally.

Maybe your roommate has found the astrological charts a basis for meditating. Some people do, I've heard.

Or maybe she's just finding a way to express her feeling that everything is connected to everything else, at least a little. It's a way of saying the universe isn't merely a random collection of unrelated things and processes.

It's a strange way to express it, that's all I can say. I have other friends—in Southern California—who are into crystals. I've got to visit them again sometime. They think the crystals can answer their hard questions.

Hard questions?

About God, and which person to date, and—you know—the things you don't have automatic answers for.

Do you still ask big questions like that?

> Not about who to date; I am happily married. But in other ways, I imagine I ask as many as you do, or more—though they may be a little different from yours.

I saw you were reading Tom Wolfe. *Bonfire of the Vanities.* I read that too. Do you like it?

> He does a great job of characterizing different groups in the city.

Yes, I wanted him to go on and take us further into more groups— Chinatown people, gay people, the arts set, Hispanics. But of course the city's too immense to take it all in, in one story. When I was in TM, Transcendental Meditation, I got a feel for the culture of India, and now I see Indians in lots of places. They seem to run every economy motel my friends and I ever stop at. Either they weren't there before, or I just didn't see them.

Getting into other religious philosophies makes you wonder how true your own culture is—the things we're supposed to believe and the ways we automatically think. How much of it is just what the culture happens to choose for you, and how much is really there? I got interested for a while in Zen. Zen is Japanese, so I found out a little about the Japanese way of thinking. Finally I moved out of that. It takes a lot of time, and I had other experiences I wanted to get. But I grew a lot while I held on to it.

> You seem to have changed perspectives pretty often. What do you call yourself now, basically?

My roommate would call herself an Aries, if you asked her. It isn't so easy for me. I guess you'd call me a hangover part of Generation X—which means my identity is up for grabs. I like to play around with the religions, as you can tell. And I like painting and what we used to call moog music; and I like dream analysis. We have a club—on dreams—that meets every month. We really come up with some neat insights that way; you'd be amazed.

> Life's pretty exciting when the future is so wide open, I guess. At least when you're young. Anymore, I think all those options

would confuse me. Do you ever feel overwhelmed by the choices? So many possibilities. Do you ever feel you're at sea without an anchor?

Don't get me talking about that side of it. You wouldn't believe how well I know what you mean. I went in to the mental health clinic last term when it all got to be too much. I thought maybe I was losing my mind. Couldn't sleep. Kept on jumping from one topic to another in my studies, without ever being able to finish anything. "What is life really about?" you know. "Is anything really true and certain—universally? How does it feel to die? Why can't I relax a little and enjoy my life for the good thing it is?" I'm not especially good at being mellow.

Some of the time I wanted to curl up and pretend there was a god in charge of it all, and in charge of me, and I could just go with the flow. Then that would seem too vague, and I'd think I needed some kind of moral responsibility to do some particular thing—but I didn't know what. Once in a while, I even thought I'd been assigned some responsibility, but I could never find out what it was, or who was assigning it.

That little episode at the clinic actually helped me some. I finally declared a major, and I do almost enjoy it for its own sake, but it gives me a little direction too. Now I'm more relaxed, learning how to take pleasure in things without having to do such hard relaxing, if you know what I mean.

> It sounds to me like you wanted a compass. In fact, I think of a stronger word—it may be too strong. A vow. You wanted a vow—like mine at marriage, and like the day when I was ordained. Those gave me duties then, organizing guidelines for my life. The vows tied me to the earth, you might say. Not in a restrictive way, but in a guiding way. I had a place to put my feet—a place on solid ground. I had this calling—to raise a family, help my spouse, serve these people of the congregation. And a place from which to look onto the world and all its textures in the day-by-day encounters with it. It made life into an intellectual and emotional adventure instead of a confusing barrage of experience. From that commitment, or that anchorage, I could risk my attempt to understand the world in depth, rather than just feeling it on the surface.

You're a minister, I guess. I haven't talked with a minister like this since I was a freshman in high school.

You think marriage vows are liberating? That, I don't get.

> Yes. I really do. It would be almost impossible to cope with all the decisions to be made in a single day if every moment were totally open and up for grabs. Do I worry about the Middle East or about my kid's toothache? Do I write the editor or call the dentist? Do I belong in the union meeting or can I relax at bridge with my friends?
>
> These things aren't spelled out by my promises, and many actions are just habit, not a commitment; but vows lie beneath my life too.

I don't think I've ever taken a vow.

> Without the vow I take in having a child, for example, I couldn't do a decent job of parenting. The work would turn out to be too hard to have any children at all. Promises enable all kinds of things to happen, as well as giving shape and moral form—what you may call restrictions, I suppose, although I see it as direction or guidance—to future actions.

My friends mostly avoid marriage vows—they do seem too restrictive.

What kind of people are in your church?

> Just about all kinds—the seekers who don't have much idea of what it's all about and some hardy souls who not only come to church every Sunday, but also confront painful and difficult circumstances with grace and faithfulness. Wonderful people. I'm very grateful to all of them.

So you have your beliefs pretty well worked out, I guess. Do they leave you any space for exploring other religions? I've thought about it, but getting into a church would seem to me terribly limiting.

> It's interesting that you say that. Because I was thinking about your life—behind all the obvious excitement, what a frustrating, painful search it must be, as well. It's kind of scary to be adrift at sea, with neither anchor nor power, once the novelty wears off.

I confess I have felt myself to be drifting, lately. I am at sea, vocationally and also in my relationship to Clyde, my boyfriend. Sometimes I want to back out of the whole enterprise of living. It isn't cowardice I don't think. And I wouldn't call it pain exactly. It's a mixture of sadness, I think, and terror. Sadness that my free search for the Spirit—some people call me a New Age freak—isn't working out as happily as I thought it would. Fear that I'm going to make this huge mistake of truncating my life, settling on something that cuts out all sorts of other great possibilities.

When I was in the infirmary, one doctor said I didn't need Valium, I needed values. Or a sober dose of prayer, she said. I told her she was off track, I enjoyed my life the way it was. But later, I began to think maybe she had a point.

I wish this flight had been longer. We're about to land. I enjoyed our talk.

So did I, a great deal. I wish you well in everything.

Discussion Questions for Chapter 11

1. Does April lack faith or have too much of it, in too many varieties?
2. What is the relationship between adventuresome growth in learning and the vowed commitment that April felt to be so restrictive?
3. What kinds of accomplishment seem to depend on commitment? Which do not?
4. Religious faith has sometimes functioned in restrictive ways, saying, "Thou shalt not" in ways both harmful and helpful. Is April right in her fears?
5. Compare Elsena and April as two young adults being sought by God and in need of help from somewhere. How could a congregation help them?
6. To your mind, are marriage vows liberating? In what ways are they like the vows we ask people to take in religious life? Are religious vows liberating? How do they facilitate the spiritual life? Do we need to put more emphasis on them?

12

Evil:
A Visit with Newt

Newt comes in for what has become a regularly scheduled conversation. He is upset.

(Newt) Whatever it was going to be, we have to change the agenda today.

> (Baker) Something else is on your mind?

My cousin Jimmie was killed last Tuesday—in an automobile accident. And nothing religious makes sense to me any more. We were fairly close, he and I. I tell you, life stinks. It's not fair. He was only thirty-seven. Left his wife and three great kids. That family is devastated. We're all devastated.

> I am so sorry.

He wasn't at fault. Nobody really was. The other car's brakes suddenly failed, so far as we can tell. His kids are seven and four and two. Joyce was a homemaker, no particular job skills up her sleeve.

> What a loss. I grieve with you. There's no way a person can prepare for this. It's different from lingering illness in an old, old man.

Well, an illness is no better. I have a friend who's dying of AIDS—he's a hemophiliac and had all those transfusions. He's not gay; hasn't been in the drug scene—if that makes any difference to you. He's simply weak and dying. The drugs—even the new ones—aren't helping him. As I say, life stinks. I don't feel like hearing any explanations or rationalizations about God and faith and all that. The whole kit and caboodle of Christian optimism is phoney.

I don't know how you do it—pretend there's comfort and hope when you have to go visit someone like Joyce, my cousin's widow. What can you say to her? Or the parents of a child with terminal leukemia. What do you say?

> I say, "I am sorry." Terribly sorry. I don't pretend to do anything. One thing for certain: I don't defend God.

I would think you had to defend God. That's your job.

> God didn't do it. God grieves, too, for the loss of that child and for the parents' pain. God cares about Joyce's loss. And yours. But I don't expect Joyce to hear that just now.

God didn't do it? Then who did? I thought we said the universe holds together in God. God is the cohering force of whatever makes the world one unified entity, the manager of everything so that centrifugal force doesn't take over and pull it all apart.

> Then, from what you say, the world fell apart in Jesus. The forces of evil pulled it apart. There on the cross the most innocent bled and struggled for breath. "My God, my God," he cried out, "why have you forsaken me?"

I know. That's true. I don't blame God. But I blame the universe, and God created the universe; isn't that so? God created a world in which the Holocaust can happen. Six million innocent women, children, and men, all of them our religious compatriots, were starved and gassed and worked and shot to death while most of the world looked on. How can a person have any faith in the midst of that, or anytime ever after?

It used to be that I liked birdsong. This morning on my pre-breakfast walk, the catbird I usually love to hear at the corner woodlot seemed only to mock me as well as the other birds. His song was hollow and meaningless.

The Bible is no help. I looked at a few psalms, all full of nonsense about praising the Lord. Praise alcohol, praise sedatives, maybe. How does a person survive times like this, a time that takes a husband from Joyce, and my cousin from me, and a leukemia-ridden child only six years old from my friends down the block? You church people say what's happening is Christ is redeeming the world. I'll tell you what happens in the real world. Horrors happen, that's what.

> Yes. And all our explanations, if we attempt them, fall flat like a blown-out balloon. Some lives seem full of these tragedies. For them our well-built world seems to suffer dry rot and to lack all purpose. Food loses taste, sex loses its appeal, strangers seem like enemies, and well-meant chatter from pious people seems either hateful or cynical.

Absolutely. I don't see any way out of it. Maybe the Stoics had something. "Endure!" There may be something in that. But not in "Believe." Not in "Trust." Not in "Love," or "Serve." That's all dishonest.

> For you, right now, it's all dishonest.

Yes. It acts as if life were good and beautiful and worth caring about. That's all suburbanite twaddle.

> There is a lot of self-deceit in people's ordinary routine. You see that when life crumbles into pieces.

> But I feel like saying, "Come on in." Join the local association of those with pain and grief and struggle. God really didn't promise us a rose garden. Almost the opposite would put it better. The garden of Eden lasted only a chapter. The rest is our world as we know it, overly supplied with ruthlessness, abrupt turns of fate, and human anguish.

Absolutely. That's a better definition than I hear in church.

> Cain is unjustly scorned. Abel is unjustly murdered.

Then the whole population is drowned almost to the extinction of the race. That's the Noah story, anyway. Then the chosen of God are sentenced to slavery in Egypt.

> And when they escape they have nothing but wilderness to live in. It's a grim picture.

Later their little kingdom is devastated and split in two and all the best of their people are exiled to Babylon. It's no wonder they desert God so often. The faithful remnant is narrowed down to one man, and he's on a cross, assuming God has abandoned him.

Maybe it is ours simply to accept this picture as the cosmic, mysterious given. Any justification of this situation comes across as hollow. Honesty prevents us from closing our eyes to the darker side.

You know, the Hindus have gods of destruction as well as the good ones. I think it might help make sense of Job to spin that out. In Job it's the devil, of course, who isn't very popular these days. You mentioned Job, so I looked at it. Job suffers all kinds of unjust grief and pain, and God doesn't answer his arguments directly at all. Finally God simply belittles him. "Who are you to question me?" he says.

Evil is ultimately beyond explanation, isn't it? I can see that conclusion in Job, and in the cross of Jesus. In the end, calculations and complaints about fairness or justice are blasphemous.

Blasphemous?

Yes. Against every holy sensibility. No attempt to understand the Holocaust by reason, or even historically, can do justice to the horror of it. None of our explanations could do justice to the victims.

Why do bad things happen to good people? Evil is; that's all. We have our games to play. I guess it's inevitable that we play them. We know we bring a lot of evil on ourselves.

And we can accept natural law. It's necessary, I suppose, if the world is to be sustained. Gravity makes the baby fall to the pavement as well as keeping the moon in orbit.

But the rest is wishfully rationalizing the unfathomable, playing games in the foothills of mountainous mysteries beyond our reach. Heaven may not mind the games, so long as we don't blame God for the evil side of fate. Better simply to see the grace in the gift of existence and pray for divine strength in the time of need. But forget the attempts to explain it.

You may be right. But the problem I see is this: Doesn't the acceptance of evil as simply *given*—not blaming God for it, and not rebelling—make us fatalists who don't fight back? Stoicism not only takes a lot of energy, screwing up our courage in the face of evil, but it drains the anger out of us. It drains the passion out, makes us bloodless, robotic.

> Good point. Whether we expected a rose garden or not, you want to see earth as a battleground. For us, as well as for God. A battleground against evil.

> I think that in joining the ranks of Christ we do participate in the battle. You know, John's Gospel opens assuming the world's darkness, not especially deploring it. The main point is that the light was coming into the world, and the world's darkness has not overcome it. We are invited to join in that fight, to participate in that oncoming light. The whole prophetic strand in scripture, and a large strand it is, fights evil. We can't be fatalists, or take the type of mystic way that lumps indiscriminately together the good and the evil.

And do you think death is in that same package? I was telling myself, thinking of Jimmie's death, that, after all, everyone dies—sooner or later. So, what's the big deal? But that didn't work either. If we don't fight it, death mocks us the more. It makes an empty, putrid trash heap of everything. It robs everything of meaning, if you let it.

> On the other hand—if you let it—death can intensify the meaning. One generation has only a limited time to fight evil and ignorance and sordidness—and premature death. It focuses our time to serve the good, to share and transmit the culture before we step aside and leave space for the next generation. Premature death does seem to be an evil, but in old age, I'm not so sure. A lot of chaplains insist we see it as a natural part of life. I'm not altogether sure about that—both sides of it are biblical.

Do you think we can have a religious faith that doesn't explain evil any better than all this? Aren't we bound to try making sense of it?

> I suppose we'll keep trying. We always have kept trying. But people have trusted God in spite of the evil. And we can do

that too. Christians have even found good coming from the cross, which is on its surface the very epitome of evil. We call that day, after all, Good Friday.

Our conversation today has been a little slower than usual. Understandably. I suppose I've been trying to absorb the shock. Maybe we've also been trying to absorb the fact of mortality, as well as that of the grief and the suffering involved in any life. Thanks for listening to me rave. Job raved at God, and I'm grateful for that. I'm glad the rabbis kept that book in the Bible. I'll bet they were tempted not to. And that book by the cynic—Ecclesiastes. That helps the balance too. Some of my friends, who are really on the outside, love that book. There's a season for everything. Life turns and turns.

Next week then.

Discussion Questions for Chapter 12

1. How should Baker respond to Newt's grief?
2. What do you believe the purpose of a funeral or memorial service is?
3. Would you say it is the pastor's job to defend God, as Newt says? How has the church been helpful to you at a time of grief?
4. Helping people mark the milestones of life—births, marriages, deaths—has long been a function of the church in which marginal believers and nonbelievers have participated. How much should the pastoral staff tailor the services to the outsiders to help them understand and participate in strictly religious work of the church—if at all?
5. How would you like Baker to interpret the theological problem of evil differently?

13

Relinquishment:
A Visit with Sophie

Sophie returns for a second conversation.

(Sophie) You were right, of course. Nothing is different. "Different yet," I should say. Because some weekend mornings I've gotten up a little earlier. Read that: "Before noon."

Nonetheless, I've gotten around, every day but one, to my reading. I chose Luke. It reads better. And I know the psalm virtually by heart. But why did you choose that one? It doesn't tell me anything. God is gone, so I can hardly think he's pursuing me to care for me or turn me around.

> (Baker) Which psalm did I suggest? Was it the 139th? Actually, I don't think religious poetry like the psalms is meant to "tell you something" in the way you mean. But never mind. You say you read in Luke?

Yes. It starts with the Christmas story, but then provides one story about the boy Jesus and then an account of him as an adult, like the other gospels.

First Jesus comes to his hometown, and he speaks in the synagogue, and they throw him out. It sounds like the problem was that he didn't heal everybody. I don't know what to make of that, but it got me thinking.

"Thinking"?

For one thing, the way those people in Jesus' time saw it, a lot of disease was attributed to demons taking over a person. I don't believe in demons, but I begin to think I ought to. Not because they're in the Bible, but because that's the way it feels to be depressed. I find myself wanting to say all kinds of things that don't feel like me. Someone else invades me and speaks in my place. I say mean things. Cruel things. Negative things about hopelessness and emptiness and despair.

And secondly, since the people in the stories sound like mentally ill people, I realized that maybe I'm sick myself. It's a better way of putting it than just saying I am discouraged. Sick in my spirit, of course, not in my body.

The powerful forces that hold you are more than emotional moods. Is that what you're saying?

Yes. "Being sick" takes me seriously. Being discouraged seems almost trivial, when demons are pounding on my door.

Then, too, sickness implies that I may not be guilty of rejecting God or something horrible. It admits that this despondency may happen to me from outside, the way a disease germ hits you. That's the way it feels. Of course, we can let ourselves get run down until we are more vulnerable to illness, and then we share the blame. But it isn't just something that's my private fault. The demons being around mean my despair is like a public health problem too. Maybe the society around me isn't very nurturing.

I can buy that.

So calling it a sickness means that you aren't healthy enough. It also means that you alone are not at fault?

Oh, I don't know. It means I'm not right, clear in at the core of me. It's not just a transient malaise. And I want to be healed, desperately, at my core. I don't think anyone who hasn't experienced it can really understand how desperately. It's something I can't do for myself.

I really began to take some of those stories to heart. Jesus healed a paralytic—well, I'm paralyzed. I feel like I am. I can't move—I have a withered hand, the way I can't get things done—like staying in bed Saturday mornings and Sundays and getting to work late all the time. I may lose my job. But it's strange. People don't know, most of them. I have this split in me—empty and dreary and depressed all the time that I'm away from work. And inside, also, while I am at work. But on the outside I can still function at the job. I can get the work accomplished. The work takes my mind off the emptiness. Did you ever have that experience?

> It's like your mind had two separate compartments—you use only one at a time. The other is sort of put on hold.

Yes. And I had another experience with Luke. Jesus teaches about the various interests we have and says they need to be organized around one thing more important. He said you can't serve God and mammon—that set me to arguing. You've got to have money—or go on welfare and be dependent on others. So I decided you have to have mammon in proportion, with one loyalty dominant. I can't go along with the way Jesus put it.

Does that make sense?

> Jesus puts it more starkly than that. But go on.

Well, that wouldn't let me off the hook. Jesus talks about priorities in other ways—in one of the parables he talks about a pearl merchant who sold all his pearls—his whole portfolio—in order to buy one big pearl of great value. Roger says it's very bad advice, at least if we apply it to our investments. (Roger's big on diversifying.) What do you make of that?

> You've done your Bible study. Where do you get all this?

Oh, my depression doesn't keep me from thinking. In fact, it may make me a little manic. Some nights I've read till well after midnight.

And for a period, as the horror was coming on two or three years ago—ever since I read Conrad, I have called my gloom "the horror"—I was overtly manic. I decided I needed to have more activity going. So I got into the garden club, and I volunteered at the hospital, and I let them appoint me program chair at the Women's

Association in church here, and I did PTA with a vengeance. It was when the kids were taking lessons—piano, dance, and hockey. I was the original soccer mom chauffeur. And I lasted about six months. I was exhausted. Came close to a nervous breakdown.

Distractions don't make a life?

Definitely not. My life didn't hang together, busy as it was. It had no coherence. I couldn't save myself with all my work, important as I still think some of those things were for our community.

And now you don't know where to turn?

No. As you say, a person can't just manufacture encouragement and faith—at least not at this level. It takes a lot more than going out to buy a new dress. That kind of suggestion makes me sick anymore. It has so little understanding of my feelings.

Let me ask you one thing. In those parables about the pearl and the treasure a man found in a field, the men had to give up something and take a risk, a big risk. Reading them, I wondered if I had too much security, rather than too little. This darkness makes me worry, interminably, about everything under the sun. Worries encompass me, like Maurice Sendak's wild things I used to read to the kids about. Only these monsters are never smiling.

Why do I worry so? We'll never go hungry; we have a home and a bank account.

Am I being told to get rid of our stuff or our wealth? You remember that story in Luke about the young aristocrat? He was puzzled about life, deeply troubled. Jesus told him to sell everything he owned. That haunts me. That wouldn't seem responsible to me, but I think sometimes I could almost do it. Like committing suicide. It definitely closes something out.

Jesus wasn't telling the young man to close out his life. There's nothing there about suicide. Actually, I think Jesus was telling him to begin his life. He was telling him to find the one thing worthy to give his life to. He said, "Come, follow me."

A few are called to saintly poverty. But all of us are called to poverty of spirit—that is, to remember that we have nothing ultimately. Everything is God's. Our lives' efforts—even these distractions—can become ways of serving God. That's the pearl, the treasure in the field.

If you want a frightening story, remember the old, old one about Abraham and Isaac. That one haunts me. It reflects a primitive time. Abraham believed he was asked by God to kill his own son to prove his faith.

I do remember it. It's one of the most horrible stories in the Bible. It's incredible to me that it wasn't cut out of scripture long ago. It's a terrible picture of faith. Don't read that one to your kids!

And yet it's there. I think it's there because there is something spiritually true about relinquishment, about giving up things that block our final loyalties.

There's no indication that Isaac blocked the way of faith for Abraham, so I may be very wrong. But that may be why the story survived. Abraham's whole race was to continue in Isaac. So Abraham—granted that you can conceive God being this way, as Abraham could—risks even that whole future, in his faithfulness. The Israelites survived as a result of God's mercy exclusively, not because of Abraham's savvy or diligence, certainly not his good parenting!

I'll look up the story again. It was so devastating the first time that I have never read it since. Simply frightful. Cruel and scary.

Like the crucifixion.

I hadn't thought of that. "Gave his beloved son." And there was no ram in the bush that time—when Jesus died. The Bible stories are all knit together, aren't they?

I'll tell you something I did think of—when the young man was told to give up his money. I am giving up things actually, unwilling as I am. My emptiness may come from actual emptiness of significant proportion.

You are giving up things?

I'm about to lose a girl to college—that's how it feels, at least. Her room at our house will be empty. And before long I'll lose my own fertility. And Roger and I are losing what we used to call our "great expectations"—the career to work for, the summer home we once dreamed of. And I have to admit I'm losing some of my attractiveness—the wrinkles show up in a mirror now, even in weak light and without my new glasses.

The way you put it, it sounds pretty depressing.

Something like this kind of attrition must come to everyone sooner or later. But they're like little deaths, nonetheless.

There is something else you are giving up, too, I think.

Which is?

The beauty of an innocent vision. You lack now the kind of naive faith you once had. It's not just settling into your forties, as you think. You believed with a kind of youthful purity once— unblemished, untempered. You probably took risks you wouldn't take today, ignored the future in ways you no longer would, reached out to strangers, tackled new things that tested you.

You have good hunches about how it used to be. It was a beautiful vision, a joyous faith, and an exciting time. But it isn't that way anymore. Now that's all dried up. I worry about getting the laundry done, getting up the energy to entertain, balancing my checkbook now and then. Where did the music go?

And God is gone, too, of course. That's the biggest loss of all.

Yes. At least God doesn't seem to be a living God anymore. Conceivably we can become deists, but not people of a living God.

What could God do that would meet your expectations, now that your life is less exuberant?

Less exuberant. Yes. When Ellen was born, I had what was probably my profoundest religious experience. I was simply overwhelmed and awestruck. Here was this tiny new life alongside me, a life that had been inside of me, a life that was a separate reality of being, with its own destiny partly wrapped up in genes to which I had contributed, but also with a separate destiny to be worked out between her and her own universe over time. The whole experience was beautiful. Alongside and within that experience, God seemed to be a vibrant presence with us. I don't have moments like that any more.

What would I have God do? Speak to me like that again, I guess.

You want to be part of creation, and instead, everything goes downhill.

I guess that's part of it. Do I have to give up that hope?

I wouldn't want you to. But I doubt you can expect exactly the same type of bliss. I think we evolve in our delights. I'm tempted to use the word mature—another moment of deep religious meaning may come, but it would be more mature, while less exciting, different, and less intense, but just as satisfying.

But what can I do?

I think you might work on in your prayer or meditation. (I guess we'll call it meditation, at present, with God so absent!)

God may be speaking in another way now—in your longing rather than in religious ecstasy like that of childbirth. For Saint Augustine this longing was God's own initiative that made us restless until we found rest in the divine presence. One of the psalms talks about the thirst we have for God. We can be grateful rather than merely frustrated by that thirsting for the holy. The psalms of thirst are chants of joy, not despair.

Secondly, your past experience of grace is real, even if its context was what you now call immature faith, and even if it's something you have to relinquish. And you're finding freedom to look back on your younger believing with some questions— that's part of a gift of grace in the present. In your present freedom, creativity may find its opening and come to help you do battle with the demons.

Grace. That's God's support for us, God's reach for us, isn't it? "Outward and visible signs of inward and spiritual grace." I remember that from somewhere.

We can use other words as well. Try using others. When youthful believing and innocent epiphanies wear thin, how then does God nurture you?

You seem to be saying it happens through pain or loss as well as ecstasy.

Some people say that if it hurts to give something up, it was clearly something of a crutch that substituted for a real faith. It hurts to let Ellen go. Letting go my clubs and service projects hurt, although

I knew I had to do it. Do you think that all of these were crutches and not worthwhile pursuits? Isaac wasn't a crutch. He was a son.

> I agree. The fact that these things are taken away, or have to be given up, doesn't invalidate them. But you come to a new stage, when your world changes. An old set of connections and tasks is replaced. They were, nonetheless, worthy enough in themselves at the time.

But we have to give up so much.

> Indeed so. Eventually, we give it all up in death. And we can always resent that too. But growing in faith till we don't resent it, relinquishing our very lives into God's hands, makes for new spiritual maturity. I see that in people who die well, if I may use that expression from an earlier time. With maturity we see through the glass a little less darkly. What we saw before is still important—like raising kids and learning a new trade when the first is obsolete. The challenges are just different.

But it's hard to make the adjustment, to give up the familiar vocation in favor of an unfamiliar one. It's so hard.

> And you're in the midst of it, the center of the tornado. Sophie, you have an amazing energy for someone who's so besieged.

A good word for how I feel. But I do believe I'll make it. You almost make it a challenge, or an adventure.

> Exploring the darkness can be an exercise of faith. Someone in despair like yours said something I'll remember a long time. "The absence of God is god enough." *who said that?*

"The absence of God is god enough." I wish I could believe that. I have plenty of the absence to go around. And so far it isn't god enough.

At any rate, it's helpful to talk. Thanks.

I'm going to memorize another psalm. I'll read up on Isaac as well as keep reading in Luke. Suggest another psalm.

> You might try Psalm 22.

Discussion Questions for Chapter 13

1. Sophie said that she might not be all to blame for her despair. She said her "illness" was partly a public health problem. She wanted to use language about demons invading her from outside rather than about mere emotion from within. Is she copping out or making a useful observation? How does her experience compare to your own "down" times?

2. Sophie reports on a time she tried to exorcise the "horror," as she called it, by getting busy in community service. She interprets her activities as distractions, unproductive of healing, but somewhat valuable, nonetheless, to the community. If such distractions don't "make a life," what pursuits will?

3. Late in the interview, Baker says, "The absence of God is god enough." What does that mean? Can the absence of God be a positive experience?

4. What are the relinquishments of your life? Of your parents' lives? Are they redemptive or spiritually unproductive? Would you characterize the relinquishments of Sophie's life as "little deaths" the way she does? Is Baker right in relating them to the giving up of a childish faith?

5. An important psychotherapist (Erik Erikson) said that the struggle of middle age is a contest between generativity and self-absorption, and the internal tensions of old age are between integrity on the one hand and bitterness or disgust on the other. If you are in either of those age brackets, how well does that describe your experience? How does faith serve to nurture integrity when the dominant reality is decline and death?

14

Buddha:
A Visit with Newt

Newt introduces a question that has been lurking in the background.

(Newt) My cousin's death led us into other things last week. I hope we can get to my Buddha question now.

> (Baker) Of course. But let me ask first, how is your cousin's wife doing? You said her name was Joyce, I think?

Yes. I think Joyce is doing remarkably well. The service was all right—a lot that I couldn't go along with, of course, but she found it comforting. Accepting imponderables like death is necessary, and the church can help. There was a lot in the service about courage for hard times, which I found meaningful. Having friends around was an enormous help.

Funerals must be a problem to ministers. We can't just dispose of a person's body and say nothing, can we? And it must be so tempting to say the things we hope for, like life after death, whether they are true or not. I'm sorry, though, the picture of heaven and our being nearer to God after death just doesn't register with me, that's all.

> I confess it's often the same for me. It is hard to know just what to say. So much of our talk is meaningless or misdirected.

> You might want to learn an interesting word sometime—
> "apophasis." It's a term in rhetoric; it means denying your in-
> tention to speak of something. That something is, nonetheless,
> hinted at, so you know what is not being spoken about!
>
> For example, out of deference to the holiness of God, apophatic
> theology refuses to say anything definitive about God. It only
> asserts things that God isn't. I try to remind myself of apophatic
> theology when I'm tempted to say too much about life after
> death—or even simply about God, for that matter.
>
> For example, I would say God is not an object like a table. God
> is not in a given place apart from being anywhere else. God is
> not a mere summation of all being, or a mere principle like
> truth. Or I might say death cannot be the stark end of a life with
> no remainder, nor is it an extension of the personality without
> change. The negatives point to the transcendent mysteries that
> God and death are more than all that.

My new word for the day. Apophasis. That must come from the
mystics. I'm not sure I like it. Sometimes theology doesn't say
things clearly enough for me. That negative way seems open to
befuddlement and obfuscation, while we're using big words.

Be that as it may, my question, dormant as it has been, but tug-
ging at me this whole time: What about Buddha?

   About Buddha?

What about him as an alternative religious leader and his religion
as a different route to salvation? People keep saying Christ is the
only way. Of course I mean more than just Buddhism, but it's a
good way to raise the issue. Doesn't Buddhism also help people
to lead better lives, help them in their spiritual well-being?

From time to time I've tried Eastern practices of meditation, and I
doubt they hurt me. I think they helped my blood pressure a good
bit more than a rousing hymn tune in a Christian church. Yet Christians say Jesus is the one and only Savior. I imagined church people
frowning over my shoulder each time I investigated Buddhism.

> I'm not sure I understand your question. Of course, if you find it
> helpful to use a practice from Buddhism—such as meditation
> —you're free to use it.

> The timid, of course, may back away from it, just as they do from foreign food. The fearful may want to protect you from alien religious influence—they may disapprove. But the Buddhist, the Muslim, and the Taoist may have found edifying habits of spiritual life that benefit us too.
>
> Actually our own tradition is plural anyway. We use the Hebrew scriptures constantly. So we already incorporate much of Judaism, if you want to put it that way. You can't separate Holy Week from the Jewish Passover. We're using more Native American music and sensibility in some of our churches. Latin American Catholicism especially has assimilated a lot from the Indians. I visited a church in Bangalore that adapted Hindu music and even a little of its philosophy.

I know. And we've borrowed from primitive religion too. Christmas was set at the time of the European pagans' solstice and took on some of those customs.

I guess the reverse can be true also. Buddhism can integrate into itself certain perspectives from Christianity. "Buddha loves me, this I know"—someone told me of hearing that among Buddhists, from our childhood hymn "Jesus loves me."

> Quite plausible. Hindus can conceive of Jesus as one more avatar, one more human appearance of the holy, alongside others. Gandhi acknowledged his profound debt to Jesus.

So Christianity can and does import foreign elements. But I'm basically wondering whether it could go further. Could it admit that Buddhism serves as a route for salvation?

> You need to define salvation. You're picturing it as a great either/or, the way we have it in a judgment day drama like Michaelangelo's wall in the Sistine Chapel. God either consigns to hell—or admits us to everlasting joy.
>
> There are alternatives to that portrayal. Salvation means a rescue from destruction. It means liberation from bondage, thanks to God. I am not sure what it means to one whose assumptions don't begin with God. To us it means, in the end, our well-being and our confidence that all is well. So I think of salvation as more collective than in that painting.

I don't follow you.

"I am involved with all mankind," said John Donne. I can't deliver my private self to heaven disregarding the hopes and well-being of people around me. So, therefore, I'm always partly saved and partly lost. I wouldn't segregate people like sheep and goats, at least not till judgment day. Christians affirm God's victory over sin. That's our experience in Christ. But that doesn't deny salvation to people outside Christianity.

Where does all this exclusive talk that puts them down come from?

Oh, our tradition has plenty of it. The New Testament concentrates on Jesus Christ as the source of salvation. Some of its writers believe that it comes no other way.

Then I am right that Christianity excludes the non-Christian from heaven?

If you were a fundamentalist and a literalist, it might. But you are neither.

Remember that the gospels and epistles reflect the communities they came out of and were written to address the needs of those communities. Tragically, the split between the synagogue and the new Gentile Christians grew larger and larger. And it grew with considerable animus. Finally the division was complete, even though Jesus was a Jew and even though there were plenty of Jewish Christians at first. So the narrower view prevailed, especially for the writers of John and the letters and Revelation.

Also, early Christians had to define their faith. Christ was too important to be received as only one among many gods. That was paganism. Christ had priority. Other gods were wrong, they said. A person had to decide. As you know from your own struggle to believe, that is still true.

Are you saying Christianity was the only way back then, but it isn't now? I still haven't sorted this out.

These days Christianity is more settled. We don't need to fight and anathematize rival world religions to make our point and to define our faith. Rather than competing, we can even think of Buddhism and other world religions as allies against the purely secular worldview, the purely materialist one.

I imagine the either/or split also comes from our tribal nature—the division of the race into "We" and "They," my clan and yours.

Yes. That makes sense.

All this helps. But put my question another way. Can't I blend the best insights of each of the religions?

That viewpoint appeals to you. And I understand. We modernists don't want to miss any options. We seem to want to try everything. We enjoy collecting religious ideas from across the landscape.

And these days we meet real people of these other groups. That was once a rare experience.

Nonetheless, the eclectic approach doesn't usually work, taking some of this and some of that. Religions are part and parcel of entire cultures. When two cultures go in opposite directions, you have to choose.

Give me an example.

Well, let us imagine a social reality troubles you deeply—say, child labor. As you understand them, Jesus and the church urge you to pray for the children and their oppressors, and—more actively—to do something if you can about the exploitation. At the same time, a Stoic or a mystic guru tells you spiritual salvation comes by way of disengagement from the world. Moral attachment, he says, wrinkles the brow and riles the peaceful soul. Spiritual detachment is a better way to nirvana, injustice being inevitable. You may then have to choose.

I can see what you're saying. But aren't we after the same thing in the end? Aren't all religions essentially the same?

A nice thought, often expressed. The trouble is, it isn't true. All religions are not the same. In the religio-cultural mix of Hinduism, for example, the time was when young Indian brides, if their husbands died, might be inwardly led or socially coerced into *suttee*—religious suicide—being burned on the same funeral pyre as their dead husbands. Suttee could be rationalized in older Indian custom, but it makes little sense for the Christian to take a neutral position about it.

And I suppose even within one religion different epochs present us with different religious perspectives. A case in point: the long and cruel years when slavery was condoned by Christianity.

> Yes. We have plenty to atone for too. But such serious issues prevent our saying religious choices make no difference.

So all religions aren't the same. How about this, then? Can't we say that all religions are just variations on the human tendency to be religious, to seek the transcendent?

> Possibly, but that generalization tells me little. I can say social-ism and capitalism are simply variations on economic activity, or tyranny and democracy variations on political style. Of itself that doesn't provide me guidance about public ownership of mineral deposits or coercive government.
>
> Religions can exhibit flagrant differences. If a religious tradition paints the physical world as evil or an illusion, it would fly in the face of the main Christian tradition. We affirm worth in the created world and related matters like art and science, sex and distributive justice, labor and learning. There have been Christian ascetics, of course, but generally we have affirmed a more earthy, hands-on compassion.

Then you do argue that Christianity is best. The others are infe-rior. I had hoped for a different answer.

> No, wrong. That's your dichotomy, not mine. I was pointing out differences. You concluded with the either/or. Your state-ment needn't follow. Truth is richer than that. As more than one seer has put it, we are usually right in what we affirm and wrong in what we deny—when we deny what someone else holds to be true. I would say that I have chosen Christianity, and that it seems best for me.

But you said religions are not all the same, and that Christianity rejects others because of their differences from us.

> Yes, although "reject" carries unnecessarily harsh connotations. It's simply good theology to realize the consistency in a coher-ent religious perspective. If an insight from Buddhist practice fits, we may absorb it, as we have so much else over time. But theology prevents us from merely collecting ideas hit-or-miss and lumping them into one.

And this makes Christ the only path to salvation, or not?

> Salvation is not mine to determine.

So Christ is the way to salvation for you, but you're not exclusive about it. God may offer salvation to others?

> Christ is the way for me, yes. And probably for you as well, ultimately. But we don't control or own Christ. We simply testify to an experience and a conviction that Jesus the Messiah has changed the world for us—and for others.

Then how about the missionaries? Haven't they assumed just that exclusivist position about non-Christians?

> Some missionaries certainly have been exclusivists. And some still are. Many others, while energetic in their dedication to Christ, have been profoundly helpful to people of other faith communities.

I'm not sure I get it. You would support a missionary movement, but not assume others are lost and need saving?

> Is that so strange? Christian belief is expansionist, for it's good news as we interpret it. But our announcement has to be altruistic, not judgmental or self-righteous. We follow a servant Messiah, the Crucified One, not a religious competitor out to win the gold in an interreligious Olympics.

The missionary impulse has troubled me. It has seemed to me like another form of imperialism or arrogance.

> And it has to many others like you. Next time you travel abroad, though, if they are around look up some missionaries of our church. They won't fit your stereotype. The nineteenth century is long past.

> We call the "we must win" attitude Christian triumphalism, and it can evolve into religious fanaticism. Fanaticism forgets that it can itself be wrong. Fanaticism can burn people at the stake to rescue their souls. Fanatic militarism destroyed Vietnamese villages to "liberate" them.

Then wasn't the whole missionary movement wrong? Surely it was based on that triumphalism. No one risks life and health the way those people did without believing that Christianity is the only true faith. You have to distort history to conclude anything else.

> On neither count will I concede. Telling others of your experience of finding bread or salvation doesn't require a conviction that there is no bread or hope elsewhere. It simply means you believe that what you have found is so profound as to be worth your witness to it, and your risk.

I guess Christians have every right to broadcast their convictions. The Coca-Cola company does it, and the State Department, and Hollywood. Christians shouldn't be gagged by their own tolerance.

> Mine is an invitational approach, you might say. Saint John put it this way: "We declare to you what we have seen and heard." We add, "Come on in and see for yourself."

This has been thought provoking and helpful. See you next week.

Discussion Questions for Chapter 14

1. Why does this Buddha question seem so important to Newt as he considers Christian believing?
2. How persuasive are Baker's arguments that one can be a follower of Jesus and still allow other religions their legitimacy?
3. How do you feel about Baker's position that the general weight of scripture is not triumphalist, but that it respects people of other religious traditions and can listen to them seriously?
4. Baker presents the "inside" view that Christianity is true, and that God addresses the whole world in Jesus the Messiah. How is it possible to believe that and not bad mouth or denigrate other religions?
5. How does your group feel about the view of salvation that Baker has—the statement that we are all always partly lost and partly saved?
6. From some points in Arabia a person can look toward both Muhammed's town of Medina and also toward Jerusalem. When the choice was made to face Mecca for prayer, in a sense the choice was made to turn away from the other two Jerusalem-based religions, Christianity and Judaism. How might history have been different if Christianity also had not turned away, facing Rome rather than Jerusalem—if, that is, Christianity and Judaism themselves had not parted ways so sharply?

15

Justice:
A Visit with Rafer

Zachary Rafer, a civic-minded and self-proclaimed nonbeliever, meets Baker in a coffee shop one morning.

(Rafer) Hello, Baker. I didn't know you frequented this dough-nut den.

May I join you? I take it you're addicted to the mid-morning re-fill?

> (Baker) Do sit down. Not quite addicted. But switching to decaf doesn't seem to keep the monkey away. It must be the sugared rolls here. I love 'em. How's business?

Not bad. In fact it's very good. This bull market is amazing. My folks' stories about the Great Depression seem more and more irrelevant. I have my savings program for the kids' college well in hand and I still have more money than I need, according to them. I don't have the energy to buy a bigger house or a faster lifestyle, though one of my friends says I ought to increase my consumerism for the sake of the community. And Rachel—my wife—says we need a summer place. My treasurer thinks it's time to expand the business again. Bigger and richer seems to be his main goal in life. I simply don't buy that. There are a lot more things to live for and put money into.

Right on. You don't have any idea how good that sounds to me, Rafe. Yours is a rare attitude these days, you know. People in this country seem obsessed with amassing wealth. Churches ought to help people find something to live for, but getting rich seems to be all some people can imagine. It's the only God they can identify.

Do you mind if I quote you in a sermon next Sunday?

Not if you leave my name out of it. But don't be too hard on people. You have a lot of generous souls at your place. I work with some of them on my day off. Right now we're doing Habitat housing. In fact, I spend my Sunday mornings sneakily topping off some of these projects when my friends are in church.

Knowing you, I realize that's neither a confession nor a boast. But don't lean on too many in my flock to join you in the Sunday shift. That housing project has a lot of appeal, and it's a valuable part of our community life. You might empty our sanctuary if you promote it too much.

Would that be so bad—if they all left to build housing for the homeless?

No, I'm kidding. You have your values, and I respect them.

Seriously, I'm discovering something else while we work. This project moves those of us who work on it to get more involved than we are with handout charity. We come to know the people on the receiving end—their problems and their economic prospects. It gets us thinking about everything from work incentives and personal motivation to large-scale social policy.

Tell me more.

Well, for example, we're learning the patterns of governmental help, way beyond what Habitat can do. People's minimum success in getting a roof over their heads shouldn't be subject to the whims of the marketplace. Having actually met people who need help, even my most conservative friends approve some violations of the capitalist dogma. And once they get the idea on housing, that opens the way for flexible attitudes toward health care and higher education too.

I think it's a better avenue toward a kinder, gentler society than the ideological raving I used to do from my socialist soapbox.

Social justice has been just about a religion for you, hasn't it, Rafer?

Very true. But you've known for a long time that I think that's what church ought to be about. I won't join the church, but when it gets into good works, and I hear about it, I can usually help out. Keep that in mind. The church can mobilize a lot of human energy. More than the United Way, I'd say. It's too bad so much is wasted on fancy buildings and the trimmings—like tea parties for the women and trumpets for the Easter ceremonials. Some churches are tax-exempt, self-indulgent clubs.

I'll not get you started by arguing about that today. It's too nice a day. You're right, though, money decisions say a lot about us. Adopting our church budget always prompts a healthy debate—How much for others and how much for ourselves is the way the activists phrase the question. We had a budget meeting just the other day. The activists are making headway. Each year the benevolences item is a bigger share of the budget.

That sounds good. But I imagine they include in benevolences some money that's just organizational, for denominational affairs rather than truly charitable ones. Those are expenditures born of self-interest, too, as I see it.

Yes, there's always some of that. But you check with church people. A lot of what you call ceremonial is supported in a generous outgoing spirit, not a self-serving one. They don't see it the way you do.

In fact, to my mind, much of the support for what you call ceremonials is given for human need too. Man doesn't live by bread alone. Soup kitchens aren't the end of it. Religion dramatizes the purposes of life. We need that interpretive side of our common life as much as we need the bread. Without it, what does all our concern for justice amount to?

I'm not sure I understand.

In this town, most of the people I meet have shelter and clothes and plenty to eat. They even have financial security. But they're very needy, nonetheless. Spiritually.

And that's why we believe the community needs the church. We need it more for that than for its social service. People join our church without much sophistication in theology or worship.

> Most of them haven't had a particularly dramatic religious ex-
> perience. They give generously the same way they would to a
> hunger appeal. They appreciate the Sunday service because it's
> some sort of spiritual mooring for them and for the community.

Interesting. So you don't think the ceremonials mislead people.
You don't think they tranquilize people when they should instead
be alerted to compassionate caring? You don't think our real need
is for justice in the world?

A rich country like ours should have no poor at all. There's plenty
to go around. The whole world should have no starving poor. But
meanwhile, supposedly conscientious people get wrapped up in
fights about pipe organs or the location of fonts and altars, while
the poor still go hungry.

> You know, Karl Marx didn't originate criticism of the religious
> establishment, Rafer. Amos, seven centuries before Christ, said
> God hated the ceremonials of the Israelites. What God wanted
> was justice and mercy.

Amos makes my point for me. Religion distracted them from the
justice-making. People's consciences would know better, if they
could let up on the God-talk and the pretense that it's doing good
to sing and pray. Generosity and jobs and fair play are far more
important.

> But religion brought us Amos. And God prompts the moral
> conscience in us all. Worshiping God was the origin of good
> conscience. You're too optimistic about human nature, Rafe. If
> God didn't teach our consciences, and if we let go religious
> belief, we could as well live in greedy paranoia as free up more
> time for good works. We aren't as likely to come up with good
> deeds as you believe we are.

> And too simple, too, I think. What if we did feed and clothe and
> shelter everyone? Would there be room left for aspiration? Would
> we then all be happy?

Actually I do think about that, you know. Usually I dismiss the
thought because it won't happen.

> And the other times?

I think that then we could at last invest much more in education
and learning. We could do more research in medicine. Sports

facilities, park lands, and landscaping could multiply enormously. Abstract basic research wouldn't have to justify itself in commercial terms so much. The whole universe is out there for space travel.

> And the churches—would we build more cathedrals, if we put our muscle into human welfare rather into prayer? Cathedrals are often condemned because they divert money from the poor. But if there were no poor, what then?

I guess you could then have your cathedrals.

> You know we may not be so far apart. You want nothing but good for the human race and collective caring, and so do I. We have a different time schedule, that's all. We divert some of our resources now—to cathedrals and such—and you want the justice now and allow for the cathedrals later. We're not coercive about worship and prayer for every last person, and you're not minding too much that we build a few cathedrals now.

No. And we both bewail the misdirection of so many resources because of greed and hate and a shabby, shallow culture.

> The difference between us remains, of course. Who determines what's misguided or shallow? You suggest worship because it seems to emasculate our concern for justice. And we think material well-being for all is only a part of human fulfillment.

I think you misread me, Baker. I don't for a moment think material well-being is the whole human story. You know I support the symphony and the liberal arts division at the college with a passion. The minute I find that parish of yours as concerned about neighborhood renewal and a fairer tax structure as it is seems to be in the debate over its new order of worship, I'll pitch in. I could almost become a believer then, because justice is what matters.

> And our lack of social activism prevents your participation?

More than that. It prevents my belief in your God. I seem to have a different one, and I suspect if Jesus were having coffee with us he might be on my side as much as on yours.

> Rafe, I have an idea. Why don't you prepare a little talk for our men's breakfast or our long–term planning board sometime? We all respect and love you; you've done so much we know about for this town. I think our people would profit a lot from

knowing you and your ideas. In your own secular way you are an Amos-type prophet.

I'll think about that. If I come, I'd like to bring my wife along and let her say some things. You've met Jane. She isn't alienated from the church as much as I am. She grew up in it and still attends a little. But she's convinced that the church has to change in its patriarchal attitudes. The language is so sexist, she says, and the concepts so outdated, that she can barely stomach it.

> Permission granted. That's even better. We're short of feminists in our congregation. Some of our women, let alone the men, reject the changed pronouns and altered hymns. And I mean just the human references to people. As to God-talk, forget it. They can't think of God in anything but masculine terms. The world in that respect is passing us by. We're out of touch.

I'm not sure it would be a peaceful meeting, especially after what you say about the sexist issues. Jane takes the language business further than you have in mind, I would bet. She talks about "the goddess." She prays to the goddess and treats her more like a partner than a creator or ruler God. It's a different theology. I confess I don't understand her—since I don't cotton to religious talk in the first place. But for her it's almost as important as social justice.

In fact, it's all tied together for her. Our disdain of the poor and the disenfranchised is part of the same hierarchical order that favors men over women. She says men have an ethic based on justice, but it's a top-down lawyer-like thing. Women base their ethic on caring.

> She may be onto something, you know. The range of concerns God requires of us is very broad. I imagine I share a lot of Jane's interests.

Well, then, if you could include Jane in the programming, I'll come, and I'm almost sure she'll join me. She's a missionary about this. I am, too, in a quieter way. I think there are some projects in this town that church folk ought to hear more about. I'll come to morning worship too. You know I don't really mind the ceremony all that much.

That's great, Rafe. You'll hear from me after I've checked around with some groups.

I hope we synchronize the doughnut stop again some morning.

Discussion Questions for Chapter 15

1. Baker tells Rafe that people are as likely to turn to evil without God as they are to turn altruistic. What do you believe about human nature? How does it relate to your understanding of Christian faith?

2. How do you interpret the basic issue between Rafe and Baker? Are they far, far apart or almost on the same wavelength in their sense of the church's calling?

3. The first churches were groups of Jews, but in the book of Acts we read about God-fearing persons who were Greek inquirers. They were not circumcised Jews, and they were not observers of the Jewish ritual law, but as it turned out they were the ones with whom lay the future of the church. How much is Zachary Rafer like them?

4. Rafer would move toward the church's life and perhaps into it if the church were more like Amos. Are there people you know who would be more likely to participate in church if it had a stronger prophetic stance? Would others participate less?

5. What do you think of Jane Rafer's division of moral concern along gender lines—the male ethics of justice and the feminine ethics of care? Can you give illustrations?

16

Grace:
A Visit with Linda

(Linda) It's a nice day out.

(Baker) Yes, I was just out for lunch.

Outside OK. How is it inside, inside yourself? Not so sunny, I imagine.

You got it. It's even heavier living without Harold than I had imagined it would be.

But I did try to do the singing you suggested—the song. Not every day, but often. And to my surprise, it helped.

"Amazing Grace"?

Yes. After being prodded by our conversation, I thought over the ways I myself might have contributed to the breakup.

And I made a list or two. The first time it was very short. But later when I did it again, I began to realize what you were talking about. Frankly, I was appalled. All these months—years really—I've been getting bitchier and more and more petty and prissy about how other people behave. I believe I've been inwardly angry at God for the restrictions he imposed on us.

Restrictions?

The law—Don't do this; don't do that. Oh, I obeyed, so that's not the problem. I was a good girl—and sweet about it. But I think that inside I resented missing out on so much. I think I resented the rules somehow at the same time I was pleasantly obeying them.

I assumed there was a real me doing God's will obediently and virtuously and happily. Now I begin to think there's another me wanting to get out from under all that. I think now that maybe in fact the restrictions are of my own making. They're not all from God. In fact, God might want me to get out from under that weight of restriction also.

You can't imagine how that's changing my relation to other people. I can no longer pretend that I know God's rules that other people are violating, and I'm not. It makes me less judgmental.

I've decided it's time I focused on what has been given to me instead of on how good I am. The exercise of making and adding to that list of gifts has gradually made the song more and more meaningful. And as a result I am beginning to amend my picture of God.

> So God is someone different from a holy set of principles or rules. God wants more from us than just obedience?

I'm beginning to think so. Obedience can take us a limited distance, but not all the way to the happiness I now believe God wants for us.

Once, when I was young, I had a spell or a breakdown when I couldn't get my homework done. I'd stay up till all hours re-doing little essays we had to write, for example, erasing, recopying, re-shaping the form of the digits and characters in my algebra lesson, making petty changes, all in an effort to be perfect. I finally came to believe the world would be destroyed if I myself didn't get everything exactly right. I got terribly sick from being so tense and from lack of sleep. I was really flipped out in mental illness. I was crazy.

Sometimes I think I may not have recovered absolutely one hundred percent. That kind of worrying has stayed with me much too long. So here I am, a pitiful, shriveled, depleted self. But I hope I'm on the edge of breaking out of those compulsive habits of mind. I still like neatness and geometric shapes and being responsible. I like trying to do good even if, in my new feeling about God, I don't have to be perfect for God to love me. But I'm beginning to understand that, as you said the last time I saw you, there's far more to faith than obedience. I think you could say I believe more than I did.

God does smile.

Yes.

> Moral awareness is mightily important. Don't disown it. But Jesus spoke of fulfilling the law. He meant the deeper intent, I think, though his words were strong—every "jot and tittle," he said.

> But Jesus knew the way we humans can distort the law to our own advantage. We can bend it if we don't trust God, and if we don't know the merciful side of God. We use it to justify ourselves or to lord it over other people. Then it's not an interest in the world's well-being any longer.

Right. That's what I did, and do. I didn't trust God much at all. My thought was to hold the moral world together. And that's partly good. But I bent it all out of shape. Righteousness was a tool I used to beat others down with.

I'm becoming more easygoing now. I believed earlier that everything could be thought out, and we could discover God's explicit prescription for everything. Should we move here or there? Should we give the fund drive $50 or $500? In every case, God had an exact answer, and we had to find it out and follow it.

> You said God smiles. I think of another way to put it now. Maybe we could also say God shrugs. He says, "Do it whichever way you like. I don't have a law for everything. I want you to experience freedom."

I never realized how much my strict upbringing had made me see God as a picky parent. "A place for absolutely everything, and absolutely everything in its place."

Now the details are more relaxed. God used to be a judge in a black robe, sitting high up on the judge's bench. Now God is more and more in colorful raiment alongside me as an advocate.

Sometimes God shrugs? I like that. So God says, "Yeah, whatever. Love me and love your neighbor, but you fill in the details." That could be a spacious, liberating experience.

> But where does what you call your shriveled faith come out after that? After God retreats from the petty details? Won't you be altogether bereft, if God shrugs, instead of telling you what you must do, moment by moment?

Strangely enough, I don't think so. It hasn't been my experience so far. I've lost a lot in the collapse of my marriage. That's what I realized so painfully right after we talked the first time. So I was doubly on my own. Harold was gone; and God was terribly angry with me. That was scary, I assure you, but I wouldn't say I'm bereft. Now I feel kind of discarded, but the freedom is a challenge and feels all right. I have a lot of growing to do.

Where God fits in now, I'm not sure. I do know that God wouldn't want me the way I've been. He wouldn't want me the way I am.

> God wouldn't want you the way you are?

God relates to the dynamic people of the earth, and I've lost my strength. God likes the doers, and I don't do anything anymore.

> I don't go along with that, Linda. Far from it. God—and this is probably what we learn from Jesus more than anything else— God cares about the ordinary people, maybe even especially about them. Jesus almost says that God bypasses the dynamic and energetic and gifted and authoritative to live with the outcasts, the humble people, the repentant—prostitutes and tax collectors and the half-breed Samaritans.

> Maybe that's what you've got all wrong. You can work out a reasonable morality without God, but I doubt we can work out that kind of compassion with intellect alone. I'm sure at least we won't be very likely to live it out without God.

I want to think about that. I'm not sure we don't need God for morality. After all, there are many moralities, from one culture to another. They can't all be right. And we need to find an answer somewhere—an authoritative answer.

> And you don't just want to say "to each his own"?

No. Definitely not. That would lead to chaos. And I don't want to invent God just because of our need—I want the truth I'd like to believe because it's true. Maybe we're created in a meaningless universe by a capricious god, or a godless nonsystem of chance. But if that's the case, we'll just have to live with it. I don't want an illusion.

> That's a courageous—and depressing—thought. Where are you going to find out?

That's exactly my big question, of course. I wish God would come in a vision and convert me.

> In time, I should think. You said you felt discarded?

Yes. Just being obedient is not nurturing. Maybe a better word is depleted. In the end, a robot would be the perfect subject of God's commands, if that were all there is to it. God wants us to be free in our choice of love for him and in our choice of obedience to holy law. I see that now. God derives joy from our joy. Does that make sense?

So I'm asking myself what my gifts are, my talents. Before, I always thought that was selfishness. But if God shrugs, as you say, if God says, "Take care of things for me," that may be scary, but it changes obedience to freedom. It could give me a calling, even if I don't know exactly what it is.

I think of my new life goal as obedient creativity. There are boundaries and tasks, but the spirit is freedom rather than necessity or compulsion.

> I know what you mean by scary. One of my close friends had a terrible time deciding between jobs. He was nervous about his ability and he was afraid he would make a wrong choice and be miserable. He thought the way ahead was to find God's prescription for his life. One of his friends helped him relax. "You'll be happy either way," he said. He helped him get over the picky image of God's governance by affirming human creativity. I guess you'd say he learned that God can shrug, as well as frown or smile. He also learned to remember that God would be out in the future with him.

I wish I had my life to live over, knowing what I do now. But at any rate, I have the rest of it to live. If Harold had not been dating someone else already, I almost think we could get back together and make a go of it. I could forgive him, now. And if that erodes the authority of my old ideas of the law, so be it. I think God is eroding them, forgiving me this way and letting me feel hopeful.

Discussion Questions for Chapter 16

1. Linda says you can't have morality without God. What do you think?
2. Baker says God shrugs, letting us fill in the details. Doesn't God "have a place for absolutely everything and want us to put absolutely everything in its place"?
3. Linda is at first afraid that forgiveness erodes the law. Later she says "so be it," when she raises the same question. How do you balance law and forgiveness in your own lives?
4. Early on, Linda argues that there has to be one morality that is right, or there is chaos. How does the world hang together when there are moralities that differ, one culture to another?
5. What other experiences may have helped Linda grow so dramatically in her Christian belief? Linda says she believes more. How could her earlier attitude be understood as a lack of belief in the compassionate God whom we know in scripture?
6. How adequate is Linda's new summary of the human assignment from God: obedient creativity?

17

Prayer:
A Visit with Newt

Newt comes back from a fishing trip with a gift for Baker. The conversation meanders toward Newt's problem with prayer.

(Newt) It was a good all-round vacation—with the kids too. And I brought you something—if it isn't too far out—maybe for your den at home. One group of Indians used it in tribal ritual. They still do.

(Baker) A bear mask. Fascinating!

It played a role in healing, they tell me.

It will go up in our den alongside an African mask we have.

Religious expression comes in all shapes and sizes doesn't it? I used to think, as a child, that all these things were pure super-stition and nothing else.

You mean you don't think that now?

No. I think that there is some religious sensibility in even the strangest expressions—in rituals that we used to call primitive or pagan. Some of it is absolutely foreign to us, I grant you—even abhorrent. I remember a small local temple in southern

India—crowded, full of an enormous black stone cow and a few devotees. My initial reaction was shock and revulsion. But then I was able to ask myself, "What is the meaning of this to them?"

You're a patient person. I'm afraid I'd keep my prejudice, if you call it that. I so prefer our own culture with its skepticism about ceremony and sacrament. I suppose that may be a handicap when I visit different churches as I do, but that's where I find myself.

A handicap? For instance?

Well, this communion business, for example. And the whole realm of prayer. When I find myself—by mistake—in church on a communion Sunday, or in a church where it's a weekly rite, my mind hearkens back to primitive blood sacrifice to the gods. They're part of the history of this rite, aren't they?

In a remote sense, I suppose so. But more immediate is the tradition of eating meals together—among friends, among disciples and teachers. That's what the eucharist brings to my mind the most—the last supper Jesus held with his disciples. You know about Passover meals and the Seder from your Jewish friends, I'm sure. The Passover celebrates liberation and deliverance.

Eucharist means thanksgiving. The language of sacrifice is there in the Lord's supper, but so, too, is the feast celebrating the great fact of what God has done for us, transforming a martyrdom into liberation for the people.

In spite of your reaction, acting out the word in the sacraments is a powerful gift to the church from God. The church has called it a mystery over and over.

I guess we can't get away from this word mystery. Science knows the sense of mystery, too, you know. But religion doesn't see it as something to be mastered the way we do. You seem content to leave it as mystery.

At any rate, we're getting to the area I wanted to talk about today.

Which is?

I don't know what to make of prayer. Prayer always seemed like superstition to me. Speaking out into an empty space as if there were someone there to listen and reply to you—how can you do that? How do you fit that into your understanding?

You've cited only one form of prayer, of course.

You mean personal speaking to God. Isn't that the most important? What else is there?

Oh, prayer has enormous range. There's unspoken prayer, the inarticulate yearning of the soul with "sighs too deep for words," as Paul put it. There's the repetitive discipline of the mantra, the phrase savored for meaning, what the counterculture would probably tag an altered state of consciousness. We call it meditation. We're learning a lot from the East nowadays, firm as our tradition is in spoken, worded prayer, like that of Jesus in Gethsemane.

Those oddball variations make prayer more accessible to me, I must say. But the problem remains. Prayer to me is a strange human activity based on nonsense.

Quite literally, I suppose it is. You don't reason your way into it with what you usually mean by sense. It isn't part of nature's force that right understanding would give you power to manipulate God.

Prayer is the watershed of believing. When we pray we've changed from analysis to worship, from what you and I have called living outside faith to living inside it. You can consider and consider giving blood, and you can take the step of going to the clinic and permitting the nurse actually to draw your blood, a different experience indeed. To pray is to shift from listening to music to the performance of it or the writing of it. It's the shift from theological quibbling to the adoration of God.

I thought we were honoring theological discussion as a useful part of mature believing. I take it that's what you do after the optical illusion flips, and you change your assumptive world— what you assume about the fundamental context of everything.

Newt, you have a strong mind and memory. Yes, one of my heroes in the faith described good theology as the intellectual love of God. It comes after conversion, as you say.

Perhaps we should say, then, that there are three states of believing. Your skeptical stage is the first. Then there is that stage
of trying it on, analytically. And then, thirdly, there is the stage
of commitment, a stage when prayer is possible. Crossing this
border into "enlanguaged" prayer is a healing experience of
freedom. We let go of the analytic distance and live in God's
presence. We live in territory hardly accessible to the Newtonian,
cause-and-effect world of the logical sciences. We live the poetic language of the psalms, which are often such great prayers.
We enter the community of trust.

You are telling me, I think, that prayer can't really be "explained,"
not rationally, from the outside. But you seem to have plenty to
say from the inside. Do I understand?

So there is no logic that can be applied? And you're skipping out
from concern for all reasoning, be it theological or scientific?

From your point of view, I am. The sociologist might allow for
the function of prayer in a human community, and a psycholo-
gist might admit a certain amount of therapeutic value. A meta-
physician might talk about a person's yielding to God his or her
minute bit of ontological reality. But interesting as these are, I
would not make a science of them, and I would not think of
them as explaining prayer or as particularly good reasons for
entering into it. I wouldn't want to calculate, for example, the
number of prayers it would take to heal a person from a specific
ailment. Sometimes I think the prayer requests a minister re-
ceives have that kind of thinking in the background.

What does that leave for the reality of prayer, then? You avoid
theological and scientific and metaphysical reasoning. What's left?

I think there is experience, mysterious as it is. Finding Christ as
God's presence still with us is like that. So, too, is our confidence in the face of death, expressed so many different ways—
as life after death, or faith in the resurrection, or simply an equa-
nimity that says, "With God, it's all right." That confidence is
something that grows on you from experience with the community—experience on the "inside."

Is prayer the same as meditation, thinking through a problem? I
could buy that—and it's a reasonable thing to do in church
isn't it?

That's not a bad place to start, I guess. Meditation is a word the secular world uses also, so it's public theology. Inside, for us, meditation takes place in God's presence, of course, while the secular world may not consciously add that detail. Meditation usually relaxes us, and it can help people physiologically and psychologically, certainly—religious or not.

You say meditation doesn't seem like an exercise of superstition to you?

No, it doesn't. I sometimes think I could even add spoken words to it and call it prayer. I use words to clarify my thinking. Thinking takes place without words, I'm sure, but not so successfully as when it can find words for the process. Thinking prevents prayer and meditation from being superstition.

I wouldn't want thinking to be the criterion for prayer, nonetheless. For the Christian—and the Jew and the Muslim, too, for that matter—prayer rests on the assumption that we live constantly in the context of God's reality. That assumption is more the result of human living than of mere cognition.

The very act of prayer makes that assertion. Prayer comes along with a certain naivete. We lay aside our querulous skepticism, entering the life of faith.

So there can be wordless prayer?

Of course.

And can there be prayer without believing?

A thoughtful question. I think so. As you've seen, believing is not always neatly to one side or the other of a continental divide. Certainly faith isn't. We're always partly trusting God, and partly failing in trust, prone to idolatries of one sort and another. The Zen Buddhist in meditation avoids an objective God of the biblical sort altogether, and yet we would willingly say he or she is praying, wouldn't we?

I think so. From this, I'm led to another question, related to your response when we first started. Do you remember? You said there was nothing I could do to work up belief in God, yet you've been talking about techniques of prayer.

Zen requires study and practice, as I understand it. It's taught. It's a discipline. Christian prayer is that way, too, I assume?

> Fair enough. In fact, the text says the disciples asked that Jesus teach them to pray, as John had taught his disciples to. And he gave them a specific pattern in the Lord's Prayer.

If that's true, using the pattern, one could evaluate a prayer. There would be criteria to measure being "good at prayer."

> I'm uncomfortable with that, as you would imagine. One would need to ask, What is the goal of prayer? Are there right qualities of language? Or levels of sincerity or truth or passion?

Are there quantifiable results? Can you take a pulse rate? Does prayer work? I could expand your list considerably.

> Of course you could. But the answer is obviously, "None of the above." Prayer is too personal, too subjective. I've heard people at a Friends' silent meeting say of a session when no one spoke at all, "That was an unusually good meeting."

> Actually, I should qualify all that. In an important sense, the liturgy undergirds prayer, and to an extent, we can evaluate liturgy. I should have stressed this much earlier. Prayer derives, really, from the liturgy of the community.

I don't follow you.

> I'm skeptical of individualist subjectivity in religious experience. Much as we may report that we have "met God" or "walked with Jesus in the garden," we need the community to temper and test our private whims. We easily bend our conceptions of the infinite, almighty Creator and Ruler of the universe to serve our petty, private interests. Alone, we operate out of an appallingly puny vision. It's better to insist that personal prayer arise out of the corporate prayer of the church.

Then you discount the private experience of God and prayer as fraudulent?

> No, but I accept them with caveats in the back of my mind. God is always only mediated to us at best—through scripture, or through the Spirit, we often say in doctrine. We need this skepticism to keep God holy, so as not to domesticate the divine.

I think you're right. How else do you argue with the arrogance that says, "I have met God, and God tells me you should give me half your wealth because I want to enjoy a life of luxury," or some crazy, self-serving thing?

And, going back a moment, liturgy, being more public, is something that can be evaluated—by theological norms, and even by students of rhetoric.

> Yes, I would say so. In the liturgy, there are theological criteria, but in personal or private prayer, I'm more concerned with the personal integrity of the prayer. The inarticulate peasant may be more truly at prayer than the educated priest.

> We could say a minister or a book of liturgy achieves clarity, or strong, emotionally moving or theologically faithful language. And we could say a leader of prayers was effective or ineffective in delivery.

You're the expert, but I want to think about that before I agree. What if the professor critic likes Bach or Mozart and despises country music, while the idiom of the particular congregation and its community is not classical guitar, but the other kind? How about shouting and charismatic behavior?

> Fair enough. You call me to humility all over again. Of course you're right—we always skew our criteria in our own favor. The criterion you are hinting at is not aesthetic, but almost moral: You want the expression to be heartfelt rather than falsely submissive to an outsider's dictum of taste. Religious practice takes on different norms according to the place and time.

My second comment is this: I think I've been quite subjective in my desire for faith, too subjective, probably, for you.

> Of course you have. That's how it starts. And only later do we come to discover that God is vastly more. I don't want to forget that faith is passionate and personal and committed. Objective assertions about God can be terribly dead and untrue. But for the sake of keeping holy things holy, I hold on to a liturgical interpretation of prayer.

One thing about your position, if I get it. Your understanding of prayer helps me with my next skeptical question, Does prayer work? With the liturgical emphasis, prayer is more an expression of the community's identity than it is an instrumental project undertaken to achieve something. Isn't that right?

> Exactly. It's something we do because, if you want to put it that way, we are told to. Or it's something God has us do. "The Spirit prays through us," Paul said. And the Spirit uses all the timeless forms of expression—homage and praise, thanksgiving and remembering, intercession and petition.

These are honest expressions of human emotion, certainly.

> Yes. In fact, prayer seems to me the most honest form of speech. Or it ought to be. Who is there to fool in prayer?

Another derivative point: I don't have to be a true believer in order to begin to pray. I can join in the performance of prayers with the congregation willy-nilly.

> Well put. There was a time when people wanted to avoid having half-believers participating in liturgical things. They would "fence the table," as they said. Communion was a reward coming after faith was reached. Yet I would see sacraments and sacramental things like prayer to be more of an avenue toward faith, expressive things that they are, gifts of God for that purpose, rather than rewards for achievement.

I'm sure our time is up. I must confess I'm amazed. I thought prayer would block my progress altogether. I hesitated to bring it up. And instead I'm thinking I can legitimately join in the public prayers and keep on with my own hesitant attempts at prayer without worrying so much about their legitimacy.

Discussion Questions for Chapter 17

1. What keeps prayer from being superstition, or is there a difference?
2. What religious history plays into your own appreciation of—or hesitation about—the Lord's supper?
3. Baker makes prayer into a litmus test of faith. Is this too strong an affirmation of a mystic side of religion? Do you think Newt will have a meaningful life of personal prayer?
4. How would you "evaluate prayer"—either yours or that of someone else?
5. Does personal prayer derive from the congregation's liturgical life, or is it the other way around?

18

Picnic:
A Visit with Everyone

Baker has gathered the inquirers of the last few chapters for a picnic on a summer evening. Present are Baker, Newt, Sophie and her husband Roger, Elsena, April and her partner Clyde, Linda, and Rafer and his wife Jane.

(Newt) Baker, that was good lasagna. And the sweet corn was superb. Must have been picked just this morning. But I think it's time for you to answer the question that's naturally on every mind in the circle. How did you prepare your guest list for this picnic? You told us to get acquainted while we ate—and we've done that. Then you asked us to try learning what we had in common. I like detective stories, and I read a lot of them. But I give up on this one. It's a mystery to me.

(Roger, Sophie's husband) Yes. I enjoy eating and meeting new people. So I'm glad to be here. But I, too, am mystified.

(Sophie) Maybe that's Baker's point—that we apparently have nothing in common. I've seen Baker experiment with groups before. We're of markedly different ages, occupations, geographical backgrounds. I think all but two of us live in this community, but even that's not total. Come clean, Baker. Are we just random friends of yours? Or is there a tie that binds us together?

145

(Baker) Well, I'll explain. I'm not trying to be cute.

In a way, April's initiative prompted this evening.

I met April on a plane trip and never expected to see her again. She kept my card, however, and out of the blue last week she called from Boulder to say she'd be in town today. That plane ride conversation had been meaningful enough that I immediately invited her to stay in one of the guest rooms here. And then next morning in my half-sleep of waking up, the idea for this get-together hatched itself quite spontaneously. And she brought her good friend Clyde along. Clyde's parents live over in Oakdale, it turns out.

In my routine work as a minister I've come to know each of you a little. I know each of you is on a particular journey, a unique journey. Some people would say simplistically that all our journeys will end in the same place. I won't say that myself. I take the struggles seriously.

It occurred to me that we might profit from an exchange of our experience along the roadways. I launched an experiment. Could we be together for an evening?

As it turned out, we were astoundingly fortunate. Providence blessed us. Everyone I called was free for today, when April was to be here, and everyone agreed to come, as a friend of mine. Some hesitated, I could tell, so I emphasize we are not to push on each other if we take on this discussion. This is not an evening for spiritual striptease or competition. It's a collective inquiry into the barriers and helps en route to faith.

Some of you would use a different word than faith. I leave it to you. Some of you may feel you have made headway, others not.

I won't force an agenda. There's no need for you to say anything. It's a pleasant evening, and we're free to continue with our rambling topic-jumping. However, if you opt for a little structure, I suggest we name the barriers first, and then see where we go.

We're a diverse group. That may make it difficult. But the next hour and a half might be helpful precisely because of our diversity. I know that I myself almost always learn from how people define faith and belief, and how they come to it.

(A quiet time.)

(Newt) Well, this kind of pause is typical of any new group. But I like your idea, Baker. And thanks, April, for your gregarious nature and for calling Baker. At least, I take it your motivation was more than getting a free bed and breakfast. I'm game for your proposal of structure, Baker. We've had a good time getting acquainted. I think we're ready for work. Maybe each person could state in a sentence or two something about the obstacles to believing—in his or her experience. First, though, I'd love to learn what that airplane conversation was about, that April would remember it so well and follow it up. She and Baker don't seem to me to be anywhere near the same wavelength.

(April) I think that conversation was too involved to be summarized. Anyway, isn't there something on the books about preacher-client privilege? Maybe when I think of something to say, I'll tell you a little about that airplane talk.

(Sophie) The greatest barrier to belief? I would nominate childish belief. I've clung to so much childhood understanding when it was time to relinquish it and move on. Adults know a lot more about the "slings and arrows." Life is fleeting and precarious. Naive childhood assurances aren't enough.

(Roger) I don't mean this the way it sounds, but I haven't had much trouble believing. I let religious mystery take care of itself and try to live with integrity the way I should, at work, where it isn't easy, and at home, where I have Sophie to help me. She's wonderful, although the last year has been kind of rough, what with her depression—as I call it—and all that.

(Newt) One of my problems is illustrated right here in Baker's assignment. Baker offers us only a vague charter for conversation. Well, that vagueness is part of the trouble I've been having in getting a handhold on Christian believing. Faith is so damned vague. I like things tied down. I suppose most engineers do. Yet you, Baker, always back away from crisp answers in our conversations. You retreat to stories or analogies or traditions that even conflict with each other. You keep pointing to images and legends as if they were important, even when they don't necessarily have any factual basis in history. Along about Easter, for example, you gave me half a dozen interpretations of Jesus Christ, and you never told me which was right.

(Sophie) Newt, what you find troublesome, I find helpful. Jesus and God and the angels were all clear-cut to me when I was little. But recently as my life seems somehow to be closing in on me, I've lost my naive acceptance of that religion of my childhood. I can't hold on to the definite pictures of heaven and miracles and all that anymore. There must be a depth and indeterminacy of mature faith that I have yet to learn. I want the certainty of having everything spelled out, and I know better at the same time. That's how my obstacle looks right now.

(Rafer) The question about a barrier is easy for me. The obstacle has been my own temptation to think I deserved my success and did it all by myself. I continually forget what advantages I had growing up and what I inherited. It makes me belittle the guy who didn't have it so easy. And it's made me sometimes hoard my money rather than give it back to be used for the public good.

(Elsena) I know what my problem has been. It's been my weaknesses—like the alcoholism that drags me down. But a woman from AA is helping an awful lot. And I think I'm getting stronger.

(Jane, Rafer's spouse) As I've said to some of you already, I stumble over the church's patriarchy, the prejudice of the church against women. That's what has most blocked what little religious appetite I've had. In my childhood church, to this day, women are not allowed to be leaders on a par with men. They're forbidden ordination. And virtually all the images of God are in male terms. I wish Jesus had been a woman. A divine revelation had to be man or woman, I suppose, if revelation was going to come as a person, but my God, we don't have to compound it by making God only masculine too. In practicing my faith, I pray to the Goddess, just to try to balance it out. And if I should happen to go to church, I change the words of the trinity, and the words to the doxology, and the words to the hymns. You look at them—they give women almost no credit, and men take it all. Sometimes I think I'll build a new church around the Virgin Mary instead of God and Christ.

(Linda) I guess my barrier has been inside. I would say it's been my super righteous, moral upbringing. I'm beginning to deal with that, I think.

(Newt) I want to expand on the obstacles I've run into. My barrier has been my confounded preoccupation with a certain kind of engineer's view of reality, one left over from my namesake, Isaac. I need poetry in my soul, and it doesn't come naturally. I think I'm on the way now, but it's terribly slow in coming.

(Sophie) In a sense, that may be a version of my religious coming of age too. This transition to more maturity is traumatic. Jesus had been a superman who could work miracles and knew the future like a fortune teller and thereafter lived on the right hand of God in heaven. God would guarantee me a life immune to pain and bad luck. Even without massive trouble of any sort, I lost all that. Then there was no God anymore. Beyond me all was void. Inside, I was hollow. It all finally left me in this tailspin of despair. So I've come to the conclusion it would have been better for me if I had been raised with a vaguer, less explicit image of God.

(Linda) But you used to be so active in church.

(Sophie) All that activity came to be empty. My healing is going to come through relinquishment of almost everything that gave me my sense of worth, I think. I'm beginning to see what the saints meant by casting ourselves utterly upon God—no works-righteousness, no religious gimmicks. Nothing. I found out I had to give up even my self-justification as a church worker and homemaker and civic activist. I'm just beginning to find my way into a faith that can accept the darkness along with the light—one that can accept the emptiness along with the fullness. To cope, I live by the very stories that you disparage, Newt. I call it my second innocence. I'm beginning to live by the stories because I see the impossibility of the kind of certainty I think you ask for. I find new meanings evolving from stories of Jesus, of Easter, Mary and Martha. And the main story—that Christ took the form of a servant and emptied himself. It's a very rich tapestry I step into. Stories now are more flexible than those dogmatic pictures I was given as a child. They are open-ended, vague in that sense. Newt, I'm coming to believe there cannot be and ought not to be in faith the kind of precision or certainty you seem to expect.

(April) What do you mean by stories? I think maybe Newt meant something different from what Sophie means.

(Newt) The garden of Eden is a story. People put a lot of store by it. But it's a myth. It's not true. And I get terribly upset when I find otherwise intelligent people saying it is.

(Linda) I think I know what Sophie means by living through stories. My journey the last few months has been a kind of revelation to me. The story I had lived by centered on a righteous and all-powerful God who laid down the Ten Commandments to show us how to live. He was a stern God, who would prevent the world's self-destruction if only people would live by the law. Living inside that story made me a tough and stern person myself. It did a lot for my perseverance and integrity. But it may also be the reason that a few months ago I ended up divorced. I won't burden you with that; that's private. Anyhow, now I've found a new story. It's a story of another side to the same God. I don't have to throw all the other story away, but this is a story of God's mercy and tenderness. It's the story of the God in one of the psalms, "who forgives all your iniquities," and "redeems our lives from destruction," who gives his son to the human race to save it. Knowing this side of God is coming slowly. My old habits of attitude don't like to die. As you can imagine, living in this story makes a huge difference in how I relate to people, what I think is important, and where I think the world ought to be going. Newt, I don't know what you would call facts behind that whole story, but it's a far better God-story for me than just the first half of it by itself—the half about law and righteousness.

(Newt) That's helpful to me. There's something that hits me as you talk. You didn't merely describe God as one who's great and good and merciful. It was more personal. You seem to say you experience the reality that God forgives your—our—iniquities and redeems us. God acts, and Jesus is part of that action. I believe Jesus existed and died on a cross. It's that present tense aspect of the story—the one that says God gives Jesus to the world to save us and gives the Spirit to sustain us—that I'm still trying to get inside of. But meanwhile I've started coming to church some. Once in a while I really find it meaningful. I think coming to faith is inseparable from being with the group of believers. I'm beginning to think there's something almost religious about hanging around church people. Worship, dull as it can be, a study group, even the potluck suppers. Faith is often a lonely quest, I suppose, for the struggling soul, but I'll bet that for most of us it's simply the slow absorption from others of a worldview that has God at the center.

(Clyde, April's partner) May I say something from the outside? You people fascinate me. I visit a group called Modern Way occasionally. They're trying to make their own spiritual way without relying on old-line religion. It's kind of like Scientology and like a philosophy of life all in one. They don't have much of this Bible stuff you seem to know so much about. Bible stories would turn them off, I think. They're big on plain-spoken truths about the contemporary world. As I understand it, they believe God speaks in their conscience, through what they call the inner wisdom. I don't hear them say God speaks through the Bible. One thing you can say, though. There's no pretending. There's no formality or ritual to hide behind. No sacramental folderol, no dressing up the priest or preacher.

(Elsena) You mean there's no music? No procession? No baptism of the babies? How can they call that a church?

(Baker) Those things are important to you, Elsena?

(Elsena) Yeah. If I take Jennie to one of these churches that's all talk, she gets bored and fusses. And so do I. But in the churches where there's something going on, it's different.

(Baker) So words don't help you? How will I preach?

(Elsena) No. But I guess we have to have words. A song without words isn't complete, or even a song, I guess. A song is more than words, though. Anyway, if God is all we say he is, you ought to have some dancing and holy hollering about it, shouldn't you? You can't take it all for granted, as if there was nothing to be excited about. Some people seem to, though. They sit all stiff in church, like they were carved out of one block of wood with the pews. I think the world is something to crow about—kids and kind people, when you find them, and sunsets.

(Jane) Elsena, I love the way you put things. I hope you find more friends in this town and settle here with us.

(Rafer) It seems to me, if we're going to talk about faith, we're going to have to talk about what's most important to us. And to me, a lot of what you've been talking about is almost trivial. Processions and ceremonies and stories and doctrine. Whether that stuff is vague or definite, one thing is clear to me, absolutely clear. What matters most—and that's part of the reason I call it my

what have you
given your life
for? —

1 is going to hell in a handbasket, not
)t it right about this or that belief, or
ial, but because they don't care about
t each other justly. The rich are getting
ed anymore—they can't spend what
they get, most of them—and the poor are staying the same or
getting poorer. This is true between the rich nations and the poor
ones, and between people in the same country. Both. Every proposal for affirmative action to right past wrongs, or for expand-
ing day care and higher minimum wages for jobs—indispensable
jobs, where you would think a living wage was to be expected—
all these get shot down because the well-off want their yachts
and casino vacations and three-car garages. The churches ought
to get on the ball and help us reshape the world toward the kingdom. Excuse me, Jane, I mean the holy commonwealth. That's
what God and Goddess mean for us in the end. If that happened,
I might believe and join up.

(Roger) Rafer, I'm not so radical as you, and I'm certainly not as
unstinting a civic worker and community reformer as you, but I
want to second what you've been saying. I'm in the church because it's good for our community and good for the people. I don't
dig all the troubles Newt has with believing; I can take the stories
or leave them; but justice and mercy seem to me too to be what it
is all about. They're something I can get my hands on. They're the
kind of thing I could conceivably give my life for, should I ever be
called on to do it.

(Baker) God forbid. I trust you won't, in the literal sense. But I
think I can understand your sentiments. The church seems almost inevitably a conservative institution, but if God is God, it
ought to be one of the most progressive and experimental of
them, working always for the human good.

(Rafer) Wouldn't it be a strategic step for the church to speak with
more of a single voice than it does? You could do that if you drew
some boundaries and kept the reactionaries out. How can these
bigots call themselves Christian, legitimately? It seems to me you
let just about anybody in who wants to come.

(Newt) Rafe, I want you to be on the inside with us, if I join up.
(And I just may do that.) But we can't make a church out of a
social philosophy. We've got to build on a conviction born of

religious experience then made into teaching about what reality
is most fundamentally. You yourself might be excluded if we drew
tighter boundaries, and I want you to feel welcome always. You
have an important conviction I want the church to hear, on the
inside.

(April) Hearing you all talk, I've just realized something. I could
have heard this same conversation almost word for word when I
was a kid in my parents' living room. A couples group used to
meet there, from their church. So what I realized is that we right
here are a lot like the church. We just don't admit it, of course. I
don't know, but maybe the church isn't people who have worked
it all out. Maybe it's people—sincere people—on the way. The
thing about church is that you have to make commitments. And
that seems terribly limiting to me. But marriage seems terribly
limiting to Clyde, too, and maybe there's a parallel. We've begun
to talk about having children, but I'm refusing until we're married. Is that just too old-fashioned? Commitments are scary. Maybe
you can deal with new ideas more creatively if you have a definite place to begin. I think it will be that way raising a child.

(Elsena) I have to make promises to myself every day—depending
on God—not to drink that day. You can't make promises like that
without God, April.

> (Baker) You know, that is kind of an exaggeration, to say we are
> the church. But it's true. As April says, the church is not people
> who have arrived. It's people headed the same way, trusting
> God all the while. I think of you all, frankly, as parishioners, and
> only two or three are officially members here. And I think April's
> comments and Elsena's are a fitting benediction for the evening,
> officially. Linger on as you like. I judge that some of you have
> more questions for each other. And there's plenty of lemonade
> and punch left yet. Thank you for coming and joining in.

(Linda) Baker, this has been a nice evening, and it's almost like
being in church again, for me. Why don't you pray for us?

> (Baker) All right.

> Blessed God, all praise be yours for this day and all the signs of
> your goodness. Holy One, Creator and Redeemer and Sustainer
> of the universe, our hearts are open to you, and we hide no
> secrets from you. Take the faulty steps we make toward you

and strengthen them. Direct them so that they may be truer; eliminate from them the distractions of pride and prejudice. Bless the people we have come to know as friends here in this circle. Bless Jennie, and all our loved ones. And bring the world" at last to its fulfillment in your commonwealth of justice and love and beauty and truth and peace. In Jesus' name we pray.

we are "the world"

Discussion Questions for Chapter 18

1. Can you define the things held in common by these people, which are probably the reasons the picnic was a success?
2. April said at the end that this was possibly like the church. Is she overly optimistic or a realist about the nature of the church? Or is she wrong in thinking the churches can say anything to the world without more unanimity than they seem to achieve?
3. How would you have stated your own discoveries about the Christian faith over the past five years if you had been at Baker's picnic and had been invited to summarize the barriers or the helps on your journey toward greater faith?
4. How would you continue the stories of any of these people if there were to be another picnic a year hence?
5. Having met these people, for whom Baker was a consultant in believing, what other persons would you have introduced had you been writing this book?
6. Newt emphasizes the communal aspect of moving forward with faith. Does he romanticize the congregation? Wouldn't some churches erode rather than strengthen his growing faith?